ADDICTION, THE BUREAU OF PRISONS AND A MOTHER'S BROKEN HEART

Denise Hansen
Addiction, The Bureau Of Prisons and a Mother's Broken Heart

Published by BooxAI

ISBN: 978-965-578-243-1

ADDICTION, THE BUREAU OF PRISONS AND A MOTHER'S BROKEN HEART

DENISE HANSEN

ADDICTION, THE BUREAU OF PRISONS AND A MOTHER'S BROKEN HEART

So many innocent children and the world we live in come crashing down on them. Shane and many other children grew up during the era of Oxycontin. I never thought in my life that so many children had died from overdoses. When a person becomes addicted to drugs, most commit crimes, whether they steal, sell, or do much worse to feed their habit. It all began when Oxycontin was manufactured in the United States. Then, in 1996 it became widely used. In 2001, it became the best-selling pain killer. The Sackler family, who owned the pharmaceutical companies, have faced lawsuits over prescriptions of addictive drugs, including Oxycontin, which played a big role, then Heroin. Presently it's pure Fentanyl. Drugs took many lives and almost my own son Shane's.

Rachael, Shane's sister, was seven years older, and they both had beautiful light thick hair and big blue eyes but different fathers. Their dads and I had blue eyes.

I called it the brown streets of Massachusetts (heroin). Marijuana seemed not to be the big drug back then, but everyone thought that pot led to other drugs. I believed it did, but today I would disagree. I came to this conclusion because some kids have addictive behavior or they hang around with the wrong crowd. I myself smoked pot when I was a teenager but never got into harder drugs. Most kids in the 70s were pot smokers or tried it. Even during Woodstock, the big music festival in August of 1969, there were films of many smoking weed. There was only a group of six to ten that I had known that had been addicted to heroin in my own surrounding city. Treatment back then was methadone, a blocker, but yet it did not help most. There were some that died.

I was a good mom; I had plenty of friends. Needless to say, I was young and enjoyed a weekend night to myself. Holidays like Thanksgiving and Christmas were always spent with my family, which included one brother and two sisters. I grew up on Herrick St. in Beverly, MA. There were no other homes but one that was set across from my house on the corner. My dad owned a duplex. There was nothing but woods and a reservoir, and then the city decided to build Beverly high school. When I was eighteen, my father sold the duplex and bought a single-family cape in Beverly. The cape was not too far from the old house. We put a built-in pool in the backyard where our children learned how to swim. When mom was alive, my family, sisters, brother, and our children, all went to her home every Sunday, where she put on the big feast, homemade ravioli, and sauce. She did everything by hand, which included rolling and kneading the dough. She taught me well. Mom always made great dinners being Italian and all. Back then, stores were not open on Sundays. Sunday was for family. When our children were born, the era of things changed dramatically.

Life was not easy for me being a single parent. I never received any financial support from Rachael or Shane's father. Both fathers were paid under the table and didn't report their income, so they got away without paying. The Department of Revenue said they could not do anything without proof of income.

Rachael and Shane had different lives. Shane went down the wrong road. His sister went in the right direction. Rachael had her partying days but never grew up addicted to anything. Today Rachael has a daughter and two grandchildren. She works forty hours at a daycare facility and also babysits at night to take care of the children. Rachael has been with her boyfriend for twenty-two years, a great guy, Kevin. She is in pretty good health. Rachael had a battle with breast cancer, but so far, all is well. She is a beautiful woman and a good soul. We have our ups and downs, but I've always been there when she needed me and will continue to do so.

Rachael thought I cared more about her brother. I never wanted her to think that. It was only because Shane had become one with this problem with drugs that most people understood. I love my daughter equally, always and forever.

Shane was an active child. He enjoyed rollerblading and skate-boarding, which he had amazing skills. Shane would ride railings and do flips, twists, and turns. I brought him to an indoor skateboard park in Peabody, where a lot of the kids went. They had high ramps that they practiced on. Shane also tried football but lost interest, and then baseball. I thought baseball would have been the sport for him. My dad would have been proud of him. Shane had just lost interest, no matter how much I tried to keep him interested. Unfortunately, his dad was not around in his life, but my dad loved watching him play soccer, which he stayed pretty much interested in for quite some time. He was great at everything and just needed more of a push, most likely a dad.

Shane was always looking around to see if his dad would show up. He always had a sad look on his face. That made me sad too. Shane always questioned me about him, and I was honest when I told him his father had problems. Rachael and Shane went through a lot with my issues of failed marriages and abuse from men, drugs, and alcohol. Rachael was a little tougher and managed to get through even though, deep inside, she had pain. Her dad had issues with alcohol and also was an absent parent.

Me and my dad watching one of Shane's soccer games.

My parents took me in when I was pregnant with Rachael. I was married to the father of Rachael then, but his drinking took a toll on me, with all his leaving disappearing for days at a time on drunken binges. After a few months, I decided to go back to her dad, and my parents were furious. I wanted to give it another shot. I had to say they were right about him, and their advice to stay away from him should have listened to their advice.

My dad and mom loved my kids, and my dad never missed Shane's sports. My dad coached baseball when he was younger. He loved seeing his grandchildren playing.

Shane's father also struggled with drug addiction at one point. I tried to do everything I could to make Shane feel good and be the best mom possible for both of my children. There were times I gave into both of them with guilt, and I should have disciplined them more than I did because Rachael and Shane only had me. I knew Rachael and Shane were both hurting inside. I did everything I could to love Shane and his older sister Rachael.

I was only nineteen when I married Rachael's dad. Rachael was born on January 9, 1978. I was twenty-three. I left Rachael's father in February of that year because of his abuse of alcohol. He went on a drinking binge. He took my car and left our newborn child. I divorced my husband a month later because of his addiction. Rachael's dad passed away years later at the age of sixty with chronic liver disease.

Shane's father straightened out later in life, but he was never the father type. He had four other boys from previous marriages, but we had never married. I could not put my daughter or my son in any harmful way with the bad choices I had made. I was in low-income housing and struggled financially for many years to support them. My mom was close to the mayor of Beverly back then and helped me move into low-income housing. Back then, there were no waiting lists. Welfare would never allow me to get ahead in the system. If you worked and made money, it would be deducted from the benefits you received. It didn't make any sense to me.

My parents were very close to my children. They did a lot to help me financially. There was one time my mother told me to go into her bottom drawer and take out a hundred dollars to buy Shane a jacket. My mother said, "Don't tell anybody." My parents adored both my children and took care of them a lot. They knew I was the needy one.

My mother passed away from cancer on May 29, 1993, at sixty-six. She lost her life too young. Shane was almost eight years old. Rachael was fifteen. They both took this very hard, for they were so close. I lived the closest to my mother and dad, so I sat by her side every day while she was sick at home and also gave my dad a break. I left nursing school to be by her side. I watched my mom's weight drop tremendously and saw the dark gray look in her eyes. That's how I knew it was the end. The cancer took over her whole body. She was wilting away, and to see this happening to my young mom was devastating to me and still is today. I was always there for both my mom and dad. I mowed his lawn, cleaned and vacuumed the pool, and weeded the garden. I took my dad to his doctor's appointments when needed. My parents were the best grandparents, and that is why today I am so grateful for them. They would have Rachael and Shane a lot, swimming in their pool and the many cookouts with family.

Rachael and Shane were very close to their grandparents and took it very hard when I had to tell them about their grandmother. Tears streamed down Rachael's face. Shane was younger and he screamed and cried. I gave Shane a book about leaves on trees to help him understand death. How leaves grow every year, and then they die. In February 2004, my dad and their grandfather passed away. They are older then but still took it hard, for they knew how much my parents were there for both my children and are both surely missed.

I met Shane's dad through friends. I lived with him for two years, from 1983 until 1985. Shane was born on June 19, 1985. I was five months pregnant when I split up from Shane's dad because of his addiction. He came home one day and pulled into the driveway. I watched and waited patiently for him from the third floor of my apartment. I threw trash bags full of his clothes out the window as soon I saw his car pull up to the long dirt driveway. He looked up to the third-floor window as he called me names, grabbed the bags, and drove off. There was no talking to him; it was useless.

Rachael and Shane always had the best Christmas. My friend, Johnny, who was always there for us, owned a Christmas tree lot. We went shopping for the trees, and there were lots to pick from. John, a tall, handsome, funny guy, always made us laugh with his jokes and cheered us up. John had also taken the three of us to Disney World. Twice we drove there, the kids were great; they would sit in the back seat of his Lincoln with their pillows in case they were tired. They both enjoyed the long ride. At Disney World, they enjoyed the characters, the space mountain, and all the fun other rides, food, and parades the second time they were older. I stood in long lines for hours at Christmas time to get a Cabbage Patch doll for Rachael and Shane's favorite Nintendo game.

With Johnny's help, we always made sure the kids had the best Christmas. Johnny and I were married, but it didn't last long. I had my reasons. We remained best friends after our divorce. Johnny remarried

. while after our divorce, but we still continued to talk and be just good friends. Johnny called me every morning and told me a funny joke. That would make my day. His passing away took a toll on me. Losing a good friend and past husband was painful. We just had issues that I surely should have worked out.

My son had many friends. Shane went skateboarding with Sean and James at Witchcraft Heights in the parking lot of the Peabody Court House while it was closed. Letters were sent to the parents telling us to bring our kids into Court for trespassing. That made the parents very upset. That's when I decided to write a letter to the mayor of Peabody, and I asked him to put it in a skateboard park as some cities already had them.

Shane and Sean having fun.

My son also played street hockey with his brother Derek and cousin Lee and rode bikes with Dave and Sean. They tried to keep themselves busy as kids do.

It took a few years for them to put the skateboard park in. By then, the kids moved up to snowboarding. My friend Maureen, Brandon's mom, and I took the boys snowboarding at Bradford and Loon Mountain. In 2001, Maureen's daughters, Shane Ouellette, and Kelly Quirk, took them to the X-Games on Mt. Snow in Vermont. That's where they met JP Walker. He is a well-known snowboarder. JP signed their snowboards. Brandon and Shane were great at snowboarding.

When Shane and some of his friends weren't snowboarding, they got into mischief as boys did. The police got involved in any little thing that could have been taken care of with a phone call to the parents. That's how it was when we were kids in school. The principal called the parents, and the parents went to school, and it was straightened out. The parents would then take it upon themselves to discipline their kids how they saw fit.

The doorway to the juvenile court had changed into a revolving door back then in 1997. The police had nothing better to do. They singled out certain kids and picked them up to meet their quotas and make the parents miserable.

In 1997 Shane hung around with his cousin Lee and also Craig. The three of them were always together. Shane's grandmother asked Shane and Lee to spend time up in her cabin in New Hampshire.

Lee (left) Craig (center) and Shane (right)

The log cabin was located in Tamworth, NH. It was set back in the woods. The cabin had the scent of an antique wooden chest filled with muddy soil. The woody scents were warm, earthly, and reassuring. They would enjoy snowboarding and ski mobiles in the snow-white mountains of NH. They also shot babe guns up in the woods.

It was Easter Sunday in 1998. I was going to my sister's house. My son was going to his dad's mom's house to be with his cousin Lee. Lee and Shane were the same age. That was when his father's mom just started seeing him. She felt that way because me and her son never married, so she refused to call him her grandson until he reached twelve. I was getting ready to leave, and I kissed my son on the cheek as he lay in his bed and told him I would pick him up later. As I backed my car out of the driveway, I realized I had forgotten something and had to go back to the house. I was hurrying up the stairs to the third floor so I wouldn't be late for my sister's. I reached the door to my apartment and walked in. I walked by my son's room. His door was ajar, and I pushed the door the rest of the way in. Shane was sitting up in his bed with the pillows propped behind him. The look on my son's face, his eyes wide opened with shock. Shane knew he was caught. He was breaking up the green clumps of green stuff from a baggie. Shane was breaking up weed. He was only twelve. I went through the roof. I was furious. I asked him, "What are you doing with that?"

Shane nervously answered, "I am only holding it for Lee so my grandmother won't find it."

I thought to myself, '*Do I believe him? Is he telling the truth? I didn't want to start Easter day on a sour note. I thought it would be best that we have a sit down when we get home so I can find out what's going on.*'

When I got home and saw my son, I sat him down and told him that it was bad to be smoking weed (marijuana), that I did not want to see him again with that stuff, and to let his cousin take care of his own problems. The two of them started hanging out a lot with each other. There had already been addicts in the family, which is not to say all families have addiction problems, but this one did. My son just started meeting new people, and most were into some kind of drugs.

My son's life started going downhill. Shane started Percocets, Vicodin, and Clonazepam at age fourteen. He was sixteen when he was taking Oxy. The pills were pink and round, with "OC" written on one side and "20" on the other, indicating a dosage of 20mg. The thirty-milligram pills were brown and round, with the same "OC" marking on one side and "30" on the other. The last set of pills, with a dosage of 40mg, were yellow and round, marked in the same way. I never found one in his possession, nor did I have any clue. Shane was going downhill smoking pot and was not sure of anything else back then. A few of his friends distanced themselves from Shane. Back then, it was mostly my son, his cousin Lee.

My son ended up in the juvenile system because of his first fight in the eighth grade on school property. The kid who started the fight was the son of a police officer. He got the best of Shane in the fight, and Shane couldn't breathe until three of Shane's friends stepped in to help. We went to Court, and Shane was put on probation, but the police officer's son didn't receive any punishment. Gee, I wonder why. That was not right. The parents could have resolved the problem.

Shane had his driver's license at sixteen and a half. His first job was delivering auto parts with a company vehicle. One afternoon he was delivering parts, and he ran a stop sign in Beverly. The Beverly Police pulled him over, and they found a water bubbler under the seat of the car. A water bubbler is another name for a bong that the smoker puts their weed in. Shane was arrested, and I had to go down to the police station. While I was standing looking through the window, I saw the lieutenant head butt my son for no reason whatsoever. I banged on the window and said, "HEY! What are you doing? He didn't do anything wrong." There was no need for that. Since he had been on probation through juvenile detention for the fight at school, they sent him to the Dorchester Detention Center for three weeks. Dorchester was a small jail with a basketball court. Shane was able to attend classes there. That was a terrible place for me to drive to. The place was dirty. The jail was not in a safe area. The water bubbler couldn't be proved one way or another, Guilty or not, for he only used the car, so they had no proof.

When Shane was seventeen, already on pills, he was pulled over on his bicycle while riding home. He just left a party where he was drinking beer with a bunch of friends up in the woods in Peabody.

Shane got nervous and took off because he had beer on his breath. He was scared because he had just gotten back from being away for three weeks he served in Dorchester. The police officer tried to grab the bike as Shane was riding away. The police officer lost his balance and tripped over his own feet. My son came home and told me the story. I went down to the Police Station. I spoke to the police officer who pulled him over and got into a disagreement with him about why Shane was stopped on his bicycle. I was so angry walking into the station because I already knew how they picked on one kid. They could have called me. They knew who he was when they pulled him over. About a month later, I got a paper in the mail saying Shane was being charged with assault and battery on the officer. We sat in front of the magistrate with the cop and Shane was found guilty. My son's lawyer told my son to plead guilty because he was already on probation. The assault and battery were dropped from his record, but assault with a dangerous weapon remained. I felt this was wrong because the bicycle was not used as an assault weapon. Why did he not come to my home and arrest him? It took a month. Why?

Mark, Shane's juvenile probation officer at the Court, sent Shane to Deer Island to be evaluated. This island is located in Boston Harbor, the house of the industry today; back then, it was the house of corrections; some were convicted of drugs, disorderly conduct, larceny, and other short-term sentences. This was not a bad place at the time. Shane's friend Craig was also there. His mother and I would go visit them together. After evaluation, Craig was sent home, but they decided to send Shane to a Leap Program in Brewster, Massachusetts. This was a boot camp for boys. They did school work, Math, English, etc... A place for troubled teens to scare them straight. I would only get to see my son every two weeks, and it took me two hours to get there. Shane was only seventeen years old then and had to stay there until he was eighteen. My son swears to this day he never touched that cop. There was also a separate charge for an air rifle (BB gun) that he and Lee brought back from his grandmother's house in New Hampshire that Shane sold for ten dollars and a skateboard. An air gun was not shot by fire. There was another charge of larceny over $250 with two other co-defendants. I believe that my son was taking pills then. I argued with the superintendent's office for kicking my son out of school at the beginning of the eleventh grade. I thought that was wrong. My son had nowhere to go and nothing to do every day but get in trouble. I blamed the system. The superintendent's office said it was the assault on a police officer that was the reason. That alone was very upsetting, knowing they would not let your child go to school. The assault was dropped, so how can that have been? Shane never finished the eleventh grade because he was no longer allowed in school. The reason was that it was a federal offense. I was very upset. Because of not being in school, the system failed him. Shane started hanging around with older kids, still using painkillers like Percocet and Vicodin.

In 2003, Shane met a girl named Brittany. He dated Brittany for a long time. I was living in Peabody at the time in a two-bedroom apartment for myself and my son until he decided to leave and move into Brittany's mom's house, which was located in Peabody also. I was forced to move to a one-bedroom apartment in Peabody because my voucher allowed me to have a one-bedroom since my son moved out. This upset me because I loved that apartment. It had a huge kitchen, and I loved having company and family, for I love to cook. Shane and Brittany both started using Heroin. Shane met some new friends, Steve, Jerry, Ro, and some others. They all became addicts, but today, Shane's best friends are doing great, but some passed away from drugs. The ones that survived tried to guide my son in the right direction, but as you know, addiction can be harder for some than others.

When I was young, Heroin addiction was around but not a big problem. Now, they just made it worse with Oxycontin. Oh yes, the big pill that costs eighty dollars on the street. One of my son's older friends introduced him to Heroin, and that was cheaper. They started sticking needles in their arms instead. That made Shane's life Hell as much as it did mine.

My father passed away in 2004 and left Shane a ring. Back then, I sold everything and moved to Florida. I lived with a great friend,

Teresa, in Winterhaven, FL., who I met in the 8th grade. I missed my family and was worried about my son's addiction. I was too far away to help. Teresa and her mom Judy were very kind to me, and I hated to leave. Teresa was upset with me leaving since she had given me a home. Every day I was worried sick about Shane. Within a month, I moved back to the New England area and got an apartment in Amesbury, MA. You should never stop worrying about your kids, no matter how old they get.

I didn't know about the flow of those drugs at that time. I had no clue. I never thought for a moment that the pills on the street were that bad, and my son ended up taking them. At this point, being a single mom, I never thought to look at the signs but just tried to find ways to support them and my own life with jobs and so on.

It was late 2004 when I called my son, and he didn't answer his phone. I went to his girlfriend's apartment, and a neighbor told me they were out selling their possessions. The door was open; I went downstairs into their bedroom and started looking through the bureau drawers. I was hoping he didn't sell the ring my dad left him. I had a feeling there was something wrong and thought it had to be drugs. While I was looking for the ring, I found syringes, and I was devastated. Never in my life would I have thought my son would be doing heroin. My life was a mess. I was running up and down the street crying, shaking, "WHY, WHY!" A friend of theirs who lived a couple of doors down came down, and I told her what I found, and she called Shane to come home. She told Shane I was there. I called the police department, but I already dropped the needles down the sewer. When the police came, I told them what I found. Shane was not home at that time. The police officer told me about some options for getting help for Shane. One of the options was to go down to the Salem District Court in Salem, Massachusetts. I was planning to issue a pink slip, which meant going to a district court where he lives, getting a warrant, and having him picked up. I was afraid he was going to hurt himself or others. I decided not to go through with it because I heard Bridgewater State Hospital wasn't very good. I was never the same after knowing this.

Shane arrived back at his girlfriend's house where he was staying. I looked at his arms. They were all blue and bruised. His eyes were glassy like mirrors. I was sick to my stomach. It was like he did not care if people knew or if anyone saw his arms like that. I could not take all this in. I took Shane home with me to where I was living in Amesbury. I made his girlfriend stay at home. I did not want them together. While he was home, I watched him go through horrible withdrawals. Shane was shaking, and he could not sleep. His eyes got bigger as he withdrew from the Heroin. Shane had diarrhea, sweats, and he was throwing up. His legs were cramping. I was a mess. I was afraid to leave him alone for a minute. Shane promised me he would never do this again.

I knew that Heroin was addictive because of my friend Timmy who passed away years ago. Timmy was a man who I cared about very deeply. Timmy's mother and I fought hard to save him. I told my son about Timmy and what happened to him, and what the drug did to him physically. I told Shane, "You have to stay with your mother." He agreed to that, but it lasted for only two weeks. Then Shane wanted to move in with his girlfriend, Brittany. They moved into an apartment on Washington Street, where we used to live, on the first floor. Dave, one of Shane's good friends, lived across the street at that time. The neighbor upstairs, a friend of mine that lived on the second floor, let them rent out a room. It was a room that went up to an attic. Shane was eighteen, so I couldn't stop him.

Leaving him and driving back to Amesbury was heartbreaking for me. I checked on him every day and night and reminded him how bad he was, knowing what I had known about heroin from Timmy's death.

I called the house and bothered the neighbor every day who rented the room to him. She got upset with me because she did not want to bother them and kept knocking on their door. It was around six pm on November 3, 2004. I called to see if I could talk to my son because neither of them answered their phones. The girl who rented it to them told me, "I'll knock this time, but I don't want to make a habit of this." There was no answer, but she assured me they were there.

I told her, "Break the door down. He's not answering his phone." I felt something was wrong. His girlfriend, hearing her knock on the door, Brittany came down from the attic and found Shane on the floor. He overdosed, and she was screaming. I heard her.

Pam was asking, "What's wrong?"

All I could hear was his girlfriend Brittany screaming, "Help him! Help him!"

I told the tenant of the apartment, "Call 911 now, don't wait. Call now."

The neighbor said his face was purple. Brittany held his head on her lap, and she kept his head turned in case he threw up so he would not choke. Brittany and another kid were upstairs in the attic. Shane stayed downstairs and kept more heroin for himself.

I was a mess. I was crying, "Let me know how he's doing." I drove eighty miles per hour down I95 to get to wherever. The police wouldn't tell me if he was alive or anything. That was mean. I finally received an answer from the Peabody Police about what hospital they took him to. Friends were calling me because they heard over the police scanner that Shane overdosed. I was a complete wreck trying to drive as fast as I could. I wondered if Shane was dead or alive. I found out Shane was taken to the Salem Hospital Emergency Room. I was crying and shaking on the way to the hospital.

As soon as I arrived at the hospital, I had to use the bathroom. I was there for at least twenty minutes. I had diarrhea from all the nerves and pains I was going through driving over there, not knowing if he lived or died. The worry, the disappointment in my son, the sickness he had, and how to help him. What can I do differently? After all the questions and the answers, I was devastated.

Shane's two best friends, Brandon and Dave, were already at the hospital waiting. Dave knew what was going on living across the street from where Shane was.

Today, Dave has a beautiful wife, a home, and two children. He had never gotten into drugs. Brandon passed away on January 7th, 2011, from drugs.

I was told when the officer arrived at the home; he immediately administered Narcan. Narcan is an opioid reversal drug that wakes you right up. The policeman told me Shane would not have survived if he had arrived two minutes later. When they administer Narcan, it wakes you up and makes you a little crazy, not knowing what is happening to you. Shane was waving his fists around, waking up. Where am I? They wanted to charge him with assault; what a joke. They charged him with heroin in his body. This is how crazy the system was. Syringes were not legal back then.

After leaving the bathroom, I went right to his room. Shane was pale and looked weak and so thin; heroin takes over your looks, body, and mostly your brain. The first thing I said to him was, "Shane, I hope the hell you learned a lesson from this. You almost died." I cried with him, and he was sad and promised me he would get help, which I heard before.

Shane was already on probation for minor stuff at the Juvenile Court in Salem. His probation officer told him, "It's either Drug Court or rehab." Shane was old enough to make up his mind. He could have refused help. Shane chose the Drug Court.

Jeff, Shane's probation officer at the Salem District Court at the time, said, "Drug Court will help him." He had to go every Wednesday. Shane was drug tested. He had to leave clean urine there every Wednesday and sit in front of the judge also with others that had addiction problems which were many. Back then, needles were not legal. Shane was charged with having the needle and having the drug in his body when he overdosed.

Drug Court Lynn Ma

While Shane was going to Drug Court every Wednesday, he met a lot of new addicts that he started hanging around with. Shane told me that being around other addicts made it worse for him. He started doing drugs again with his new friends from Lynn. This is why today he

20

refuses to go to NA (Narcotics Anonymous) or any other programs. He is better off not being around them.

Shane failed one of the drug screens, and the judge sent him to a holding facility in Tewksbury. There he had to wait for the availability of a bed. It took months to get a bed. Many could not find beds.

Then Shane ended up with a toothache, and Brittany brought him to the dentist. Shane was given Vicodin for his tooth. Shane knew he would test positive and went on the run. For months Shane and his girlfriend were on the lam. There was a warrant out for Shane's arrest.

I knew my son was a mess, and I was scared to death that Shane was going to die. I had no idea where Shane was staying or if he was staying with someone or in the street. Shane would call me. His words would be slurring, and the way he said, "Ya, Mom." I always knew he was high. Shane never made sense with his words, or he'd just agree with me about anything. "Ya Mom" was a dead giveaway. Shane would just hang his phone up on me because he was so out of it. As his mother, I just knew he was high. I couldn't sleep at night. I was afraid the phone would ring, and I would get the bad news. I couldn't turn my phone off.

Shane's guilt got the best of him when he was messed up. He had to call me when he was coming down off the high. Shane knew he was hurting the ones he loved. Friends were calling me and telling me Shane looked terrible from the drugs.

I couldn't hold down a job. I was always running out of work, worrying if he was dead or alive. I had no one to lean on. Not even his father was ever there for him. I called the Police Department in Peabody and asked the sergeant, who today is a captain, to help track Shane down because I did not want my son to die. Shane was finally picked up in Peabody Square with counterfeit money; it was a setup, meaning if it was not for Captain Richards, my son would probably not have made it and overdosed somewhere. He ended up doing six months in Middleton. From there, Shane was sent to Lawrence Farm. Lawrence Farm is a correctional facility but with more freedom. It was a big brick building set back off the highway. They would go out and clean up the trash on the sides of the highways and wash confetti off the walls, and also shooted heroin. These prisons and wherever they were sent, they could never escape from drug use. Britt and I visited Shane on the weekends. There would be picnic tables outside, and we go grab one after being approved at the guard gate. One day Shane was given Vicodin by a guard, and I reported that to the head of the prison. He had told me what made him relapse in the first place while he was there.

Then Shane was sent back to Middleton, a county jail known for its strictness. He was placed in segregation, also known as "the hole," for thirty days during the middle of the summer. During his time in the hundred-degree hole, I received a letter from Shane, and it was so upsetting. During the hot summer months, they made him sleep on wet sheets from the sweat that poured off his skin. Shane put a towel in the window to block the sun from coming in. Then the guard would go into the cell and take it down. He was treated like an animal there. I was so upset I called the sheriff, and I told him how I felt about it, how wrong it was. The sheriff said, "No one should be treated like that."

I replied, "My son was." The sheriff fixed that problem. After thirty days in the hole, Shane went back to 80 Beds (the drug unit in the Middleton House of Corrections). This was a unit where the addicts were dealt with. Drugs still got in the jails by men putting the heroin up their rectum, and then they would wait to defecate.

Shane never had problems with women, but his problem was way worse than losing relationships.

Because of my son relapsing, Brittany decided to move on with her life. She wrote Shane a letter and broke up with him. It was upsetting for Shane to get that letter. Brittany today turned her life around, divorced with children and doing well for years, clean and sober.

After Shane finished serving his seven months, he went back to his old self, still in Drug Court, meeting new friends. Shane skipped one Wednesday at Drug Court. I was waiting for him outside, but he took off in a car with his future son's mother. They stayed together for the next five years. The two of them lived in three different apartments,

nd the last one was in Beverly. They had a great relationship and got
along really well. Shane stuck to his old habit and started hanging
around with new people. One of his closest friends was Jerry, who
once dated Jeanette's sister.

One night in Lynn in 2006, Shane was running across the street.
He was stopped by the police, and he was searched. They found a
bag of heroin and $410 cash on him. Shane was brought to the Lynn
Court House. I tried to get help for him instead of him going to jail.
There was no talking to this judge. Shane was sentenced to a year in
the Middleton House of Corrections again. He served seven months
out of that year. Jeannette and I visited him every weekend. During
the time he was away, I was very upset about addicts being put in
jail instead of them getting the help they needed, so I wrote a
personal letter to District Attorney Blodgett's Office and also to the
editor.

Better Ways to Deal with Drug Problems

"I am writing about the epidemic of Oxycontin on the North Shore.
Let me just say that it is everywhere. My personal opinion is that it is
not Oxy. It has progressed to Heroin, and our children are dying from it
every day.

A lot of parents are burying their children at a young age because
of this scourge that ruins the lives of those that are left behind.

Jail doesn't seem to be the answer. Why can't the money spent on
incarceration be used to provide rehabilitation beds in all halfway
houses, where some tools for rejoining society in a sober, productive
manner can be taught?

Peer pressure may be the cause of developing drug dependency. I
feel that jail is no deterrent as it only increases depression.

Please, can we remake the present system of arrest, court, jail, and
probation into something that goes like arrest, court, and rehabilitation
in community service time in classrooms or hospitals? This or are we
going to leave it as is: Jail full, rampant sales and usage on the streets,

young people dying, lives ruined? Will this be the legacy we deed to our grandchildren?"

I never received any decent response to that letter, so I decided to organize a vigil for drug awareness. Before that, at one point, Maureen (Brandon's mom) and I went to a vigil in Lynn. I thought it was a good idea to have one in Peabody because there were so many overdoses in Peabody, Massachusetts.

I called Salem News and asked if they would do a story with me on drug awareness. I talked to Julie at the Salem News. She came to the salon where I worked and did an interview with me.

In September of 2006, I was interviewed by Salem News. Here are a couple of articles from the paper.

Denise Hansen holding a picture of her son Shane.

Mother Organizes Vigil to Raise Drug Awareness Oct. 8, 2006.

PEABODY- Denise Hansen is fighting for her son's life.

Every time the subject of her 21-year-old's opioid addiction comes up, the hairdresser's eyes well up.

Denise said, "I never thought in a million years my son would do heroin."

At eighteen, Shane Hansen narrowly escaped death by an overdose. His addiction has taken him on a roller coaster ride with more than a few stops in jail. Since June, he's been serving time in the Middleton Jail.

Now, his mother wants to do something to raise awareness about the deadly array of drugs known as opioids. She is organizing a candle-light vigil next month for the victims of the North Shore's drug scourge, their families, and their friends.

Denise Hansen wants to read the name of every person in the area who has died from overdosing on drugs like OxyContin and Heroin. She, along with other parents and family members of drug addicts, will speak about the toll the drugs have taken on their lives.

"I just got to pray. This has been four years of hell," said Hansen, a fifty-one-year-old mother of two. "That's why I'm doing the vigil. I love him."

Her goals are not lofty. She just wants kids to understand the real danger of drugs. Denise wants the parents to know her story so they can get help sooner. She hopes drug makers will stop producing such addictive drugs.

Hansen described her son as loving, and she held a photo of her and her son while she was being interviewed. They're both smiling. "He's a good-hearted kid. I want everyone to know about drug aware-ness," she said.

She knows that for Shane to leave behind his life of drugs, he must permanently part ways with his circle of friends and get a job. She also understands that it is difficult for a man who was not allowed to ever finish school.

Road to addiction (Salem News)

Denise Hansen will never forget the day she got that hysterical call from Shane's girlfriend, Brittany. Her son had overdosed on heroin. It was Nov. 3, 2004.

"It was the most horrible experience in my life," Denise said. "Thank God he made it through." Shane had to submit to a regular schedule of drug testing every Wednesday. If he failed, he would have to do a brief stint in jail. He would clean up but quickly relapse.

He recently wrote a letter to his mother about his addiction, his entry into drugs, his denial of his addiction, the skin-crawling nature of withdrawal, and his fear of turning around.

Life for Shane had rarely been easy. His father had little but none to do with him because he struggled with his cocaine addiction. "That's why I left him." I raised Shane and his older sister Rachael as a single mother. They had different fathers, and I had moved around a lot when the kids were little.

"I was back and forth from Danvers to Salem to Peabody," Denise Hansen said.

Rachael, 28, was then single. "She's fine. She's great," Denise said. "She works with children."

By the time the family moved to Peabody permanently and changed to middle school, Shane had obvious behavioral problems.

I asked Shane to write me that letter while he was incarcerated. Shane sent me the letter, and I believed every word of it. This gave me the strength to fight against drugs so they would get the treatment they needed instead of going to jail. Then, I asked my friend Maureen Ouellette to help me with a vigil in Peabody because her son Brandon just started using drugs. Brandon was good friends with Shane. Shane had many other friends that were also addicted that he hung around with. I felt that if you hung around with dogs that had fleas, you would get fleas.

I put all my efforts into this vigil and went to the committee in Peabody City Hall. I asked if we could hold the vigil in the Commons. The committee agreed, and they allowed me to do it. Maureen and I went to a vigil the month before in the Lynn Commons. I thought Peabody needed to have this awareness because they lost hundreds of kids from overdoses.

After that, I decided to have a community awareness and vigil here at the Peabody Commons. I felt so dedicated and worked hard. The vigil was held on October 8, 2006. Shane allowed me to put his picture on the front page of the newspaper for drug awareness. Back then, we read hundreds of names that had overdosed, and some were my son's friends. We had the late State Representative Joyce Spilliotis present, the Peabody City Hall councilors, Peabody police, Ann from Seth Moulton's office, and Joan Lovely, our state rep, and to tell the Mayor and the DA to fight for more beds and rehabilitation instead of incarceration. I wrote many letters to State Reps in the newspaper. A hundred people showed up for the vigil.

I wrote many letters to State Representatives and the newspaper. People called me and wanted to speak at the vigil. I heard from two women and a man who both lost two of their children. Another one of my son's friend's mothers who lost their son also spoke.

Shane's father's mother donated flowers to put on the platform. On the day of the vigil, I started my speech:

"Hello, my name is Denise Hansen; I am the mother of a Heroin addict. His name is Shane, and he is now twenty-one years old. He started with Percocet, then Oxycontin at sixteen. That turned him to Heroin because it was cheaper.

Shane overdosed in 2004 and was administered Narcan. It saved his life, but it didn't end there. Soon after, Shane wanted to try Drug Court. Shane missed some sessions. He was arrested for possession of a gram of heroin and sentenced to a year in jail. I asked for treatment, but the judge said, "No." I felt that jail was not the answer.

Sergeant Scott Richards was there. I thanked him for getting my son off the streets. I would call him even if he had to be arrested in order to save his life.

Back then, we read hundreds of names that had overdosed, and some were my son's friends. I wrote many letters to State Reps in the newspaper. I proceeded to read my son's letter to all of them.

Shane's Letter: Addiction to Drugs by Shane Hansen

"I spent part of my life in Danvers. I have always loved aggressive sports like rollerblading, skateboarding, and riding bikes. Sports were my life. There were no places to go for rollerblading and skateboarding, so we were always getting in trouble. The police summoned us to court for trespassing. I started getting in trouble for selling a BB gun for a skateboard and $10. I was hanging out with the wrong crowd of people. I soon gave up on sports that I loved and that I spent so much time doing. I started smoking marijuana and drinking for a long period when I was only fourteen. I would not go anywhere without my weed. I had a very abusive, compulsive behavior with anything. In Middle School, I was in a behavior classroom. They did not want me anywhere else in the school because I was always getting into trouble. It got so bad I was being bribed with money and other things to be good. The housemaster paid for me to go on a field trip to Washington, DC, to Peabody Higgins School after moving there. They kicked me out of alternative school and then the good with the federal offense against the police officer. I was in and out of DAYS from 17 to 18 years old. Then came adult jails and how to drugs and more problems. I was looking up to older people and taking after them. I started selling weed so I could make easy money and support my habits. Then, it was the Benzos, Percocet, and Vicodin. I found myself doing whatever I could for money and drugs. Whoever had a lot of money and drugs, my friends and I found a way to get our hands on it. We did not care if we had to risk our lives to do what we had to do. We did not think twice. We just did it. Robbing, cheating, stealing, and lying. If there was someone to get over on, we got over on them. I soon found Oxycontin. I looked at it just like another pill, like Perc or Vicodin. I got my hands on some of them, dealing with them, crushing them, and snorting them. That is where I found my new love. There was nothing else I could've found better. I never knew if I tried to stop, I would've been so sick. I didn't know what was wrong, but I knew it was the most uncomfortable feeling ever. I wanted to crawl out of my skin. I did not want to feel like that again, so what I did was get more and do whatever I had to do. The Oxy led right to snorting and getting in trouble, stealing, lying, and cheating. I soon went to an adult jail, being on probation from when I was 15 years old. When I was young, I always wanted to grow up quickly, and now that I'm older, I feel the opposite. I overdosed when I was seconds away from dying. It did not register in my mind how close I was to death. My whole life started to fall apart more y the day. I was hurting everyone that cared about me, and I didn't even care. I was digging myself deeper and deeper into my own grave. would get out of jail and try to play the system again, giving fake urines, lying to everyone, and telling them I was clean when I was not. No one could try to tell me any different. I was scared to change; I was afraid to change. The only thing I knew was how I was living in crim-nal thinking, the very same hassle of running on the streets. I did not know how to live any other way. I love to use it and use it to live. I will end up back in jail dope sick. Your body doesn't feel normal for at least a month. After all that, you have to deal with the reality of all the pain and misery you don't have when you use it because all that goes away temporarily by getting high. You just ported to the side for another day, and it all just builds up inside of you. You realize all the people you hurt and all the people who try to help. The most for it is on yourself. Some people give up on you because of the problem you cause. We use it as an excuse to get high more and higher. Now, I find myself sitting back in jail, knowing I am still alive but have another run in me. The question is, Do I have another recovery in me that I have to start now because I might not be alive through my next run? I know all the energy I put into hustling and getting high needs to be put into staying sober."

The parents all spoke of the loss of their children. We lit candles and read off a little more than two hundred names of people that passed away. Everyone was sitting on the Commons grass listening, and some were crying. A friend played the organ. I cannot recall the song, but it really was a beautiful tune for the ones of families that lost loved ones from addiction. The vigil sheds light on the dangers of drugs. One woman, Joan, spoke of losing her two beautiful daughters, and Mr. Rosa lost his two sons. Also, Debra lost her son two blocks from the Sober house in Boston. I also thanked Maureen Ouellette and her daughter Shane for helping me that day. Maureen spoke about her son Brandon who was going down the wrong path. I thanked everyone else that came that day.

They started talking about legalizing syringes in 2007. The newspaper asked me my opinion, and I said, "ABSOLUTELY NOT! This enables them. Why don't you just put the dope in the needle for them?'

Shane was released in 2007, and he reunited with Jeanette.

Shane stayed with my friend Billy at his house. Shane's girlfriend spent

many nights there with Shane.

His son Cody was born on January 20, 2008. Shane struggled at the Methadone Clinic, and it had put some weight on him. That's what the medication does to some people. Methadone is just another pacifier. I believe that the legalization of syringes in 2007 it was enabling addicts to use more. The overdoses skyrocketed, and they killed more people than HIV alone. My son tells me today that the addicts share the syringes, so it doesn't matter where they get them. Now, we have a cure for HEP C. When Shane was released, he started using Heroin again. I could always tell by his eyes and the way he talked to me. He was absent from our family gatherings. Shane knew it was time to get help.

Back then, Shane had the responsibility of his son. Shane

went to the methadone clinic for three years. I learned more about the drug over time. Shane skipped doses, used Heroin, and then used the clinic so he wouldn't get sick. The clinic would show he relapsed but would slap him on the wrist and say, "Just come back."

Shane developed a $250/day habit. In 2008-2009 Shane was living in Beverly with his son and Jeannette right downtown. They had a beautiful two-bedroom apartment. They had two Pit Bulls (Cypress and Chaos). They were great dogs. I went over there and walked them every day.

I noticed Shane and his girlfriend were getting a lot of nice things, and I had the gut feeling something was up. Jeannette tried. She loved Shane, but she was not a user. All the gold Shane had made me wonder. Jeannette was not sure what was going on with him. She eventually caught on.

While living in Beverly, Shane received three different charges. At one of my visits to walk the dogs, Shane asked me to babysit his son.

Jeannette was not home. She had no clue. Shane told me he got called into work. I was suspicious. I said to him, "I hope you're not dealing drugs or anything because if you are, you'll end up losing everything you've got." He lied to me. I received a phone call from him from the Salem Police Station. He was charged with intent to distribute in Salem with two other friends. One friend he met at Drug Court, and the other one was a childhood friend. The second time was when a friend from Gloucester set him up to sell Cocaine to an undercover cop in Beverly. The kid who set him up was also arrested a month earlier and set my son up to get him a lighter sentence. The police did not arrest Shane at that time because they were doing surveillance on his house every day. Shane got word the heat was on. Jeannette and his son moved out and moved in with her mother. She remained Shane's girlfriend. Jeanette continued to stay nights with Shane at their apartment.

In February 2009, the door to Shane's apartment was broken down by the cops. They raided the house with a warrant. Cypress ran away, and the other dog lapped the policeman's foot. Shane's pit bulls were around three years old then. My girlfriend Betty and I were interrupted while watching a movie. Jeanette called me on the phone to get over there fast. The cops were at the house arresting Shane. I ran over there. The cops broke the door right off the hinges, and they wouldn't let me in the house; I had to wait outside. The cops were hoping to find lots of drugs, but they did not. They arrested him for the drug charges from two months before for the cocaine. The cops roughed Shane up, pepper-sprayed him in the face. There was no reason for it. This was all done in front of their one-year-old son. Jeanette said, "Shane never resisted arrest." There was blood all over the kitchen floor. There was blood of Shane all over the dogs' beds. I had taken photos of it all and given it to his lawyer.

Cody was picked up by his maternal grandmother. I stayed that night with my grandson's mother because the door was wide open. His girlfriend and I went looking for Cypress. Cypress came home at 4 am. I heard her at the door crying. The next day Jeannette permanently moved back in with her mother. We went to Court the next morning for

Shane's arraignment, and he got a $5,000 bail. I sold all of Shane's gold jewelry and all of his other stuff. I filed Shane's tax returns and got the security deposit back from the apartment. That gave me the $5,000 for the bail money. I had the dogs with me for a while, and I had to find a good home for them. I interviewed some people from Craig's list. I slept on an inflatable mattress with both dogs while I cleaned out the apartment. I did this all by myself. Then I found Janessa and John from Salem. I did not want the dogs abused. They first took Cypress (the female) and then decided to take Chaos, for I had found someone else, and he tried to sell Chaos on the internet; that is where I had the Peabody police help me get him back from that person because I knew where his home was for I checked it out. They lied and tried to tell me they did not know where he was. That one Peabody police officer called me back, and thank God, he met me and got me back. Janessa and John took Chaos into their home also. They were the kindest people you could ever meet. They moved to George-town in a house with a big yard. Chaos (the male) passed away in 2018 at age eleven. Cypress was alive at that time but died at age 14; I got to say goodbye to her. I still keep in touch with Janessa and John today.

Once Shane was bailed out, he went on the run. Shane's baby's mother was in and out of their relationship then. Shane was hanging out with a friend named Tammy. They were out one night, and Shane received a text from his father's girlfriend. Shane read the text, and his truck swerved a little. He was pulled over by the Peabody Police. Shane was given a breathalyzer, and this time it read over 3.0. Shane had only one drink. One police officer was going to let him go, but the other said, "We just arrested his father tonight. Let's take him in."

Shane shoved the cop out of the way. Tammy kicked the truck door open so Shane could get back in the truck. They took off. The night this happened, it was a rainy night, the dogs were looking for him, and Peabody police seemed to always have it out for him. I spoke to him on the phone, and he told me where he was, which was in the bushes of a complex in Salem. He asked me to direct the police somewhere else so he could get away because of the dogs, and I just did that. Lucky for him, it was raining that night, and dogs could not sniff them out. I Had no trust in some of the police officers. The dogs scared the hell out of me. Maybe I was wrong, but I believed they should have never arrested him at that time, for my son was never much of a drinker.

Shane's lawyer told me he would lose his bail money if he didn't turn himself in. Salem Police officer that helped me before. He was the one who arrested Shane before for intent to distribute. Shane's lawyer said, "That's when I asked the Salem Officer from Salem who knew Shane from his last arrest because he knew what kind of car Shane was driving around in. I knew where that car was at a Beverly home. There was a rumor going around that the Peabody Police would beat him up if they found him. It was all I heard, but I was worried they did not like my son. The Salem Police asked the Beverly Police to pick him up at the Beverly home, where he was hiding in a closet. They arrested him and took him to the Middleton Jail overnight. In the morning, Shane went to the courthouse for his arraignment, and while the lawyer and I were waiting upstairs for him to come up, he was caught on camera snorting heroin because they never searched him when he was arrested. I was devastated; I KNEW HOW SICK HE WAS. He was denied bail. The lawyer said, "This is the first time his lawyer ever told a judge we don't want any bail." If I hadn't helped the Salem cops find Shane and had him picked up, he would have lost his bail money. That's when I asked his lawyer, "Can he please go to rehab? He needs help, not jail."

The lawyer replied, "The judge will deny it."

Shane was held without bail.

I worked publicly to try to decrease the area's drug problem, and I organized a candlelight vigil. My son has struggled with drug addiction since his teens. Shane had gone to Superior Court in Salem in front of Judge Feeley. The judge sentenced him to three years for the charges he had. Shane served his time at Donald W. Wyatt Detention Center in Central Falls, Rhode Island. In 2019, I went to a rally in front of the Salem District Court House. It concerned a judge that let an immigrant get just probation for selling Heroin and Fentanyl. I wrote this letter to the editor concerning Judge Feeley sparing the heroin dealer from jail.

This was my article to the editor: I am writing regarding the article on May 16th titled "Judge spares heroin dealer from jail." This made me furious to hear that Judge Timothy Feeley sentenced 32-year-old man Manuel Soto-Vittini to two years probation for drug possession with intent to distribute. Soto-Vittini claimed he was just selling to provide for his family. He was here on a green card.

That same judge sentenced my son to three years in state prison for distributing Cocaine to an undercover cop and snorting Heroin in the bathroom of the courthouse while waiting to see the judge. The difference is my son has been a heroin addict since 2003. Heroin addicts have a disease that makes them make wrong decisions and bad choices. Soto-Vittini (a dealer who made people addicted and ruined families) was in his right mind. Addicts sell drugs to support their habit because they are sick. Soto-Vittini sold them to make money to help his family, and Judge Feeley felt that was okay.

What about my family and all other families that lost their kids to drugs? I wanted rehabilitation for my son instead of jail at the time and got nothing. The state and federal levels are so unjust, and something should be done. Judge Timothy Feeley should be taken off the bench. Maybe he's a Trump hater because Soto-Vittini gets probation as a dealer only, and others, like addicts, get serious time. There's no justice there. I, as his mom, fought hard back then for treatment. Still, to this day, all the letters and advocating I did, they are still today 2023 on the streets, homeless people are shooting up, and not enough treatment centers are built to help them.

During his sentence, his son's mother and I would take his son to visit him every weekend. There were times I went alone.

Me visiting Shane with his son.

Visiting Daddy.

Shane served 2 ½ years, and the last six months of it was probation. The mother of my grandson moved in with me in Apple Village in

Beverly. They stayed with me in a one-bedroom apartment for six months. Then I transferred to a three-bedroom townhouse so my grandson could have his own room. We lived together for three years Jeanette and I had our ups and downs. I took care of my grandson while she worked and went to school. I took my grandson on the bus with me while I was working, picking up and dropping off kids at their school.

Ten months before Shane's release, Jeanette had a relationship with another man. Then she became pregnant. So I moved to a one-bedroom apartment down the street. I let them remain there in the three-bedroom townhouse so my grandson would have stability. My grandson and I became close.

Shane was released on parole in June after serving 2 ½ years. My friend Billy allowed him to be paroled to his house for the last six months of that sentence which ended on December 31, 2011. Billy, my dear friend, had a ranch home with a big yard and pool, and two extra bedrooms.

I found two different good-paying jobs for Shane. A real good friend of mine, Jeremy, whom I knew from karate which I had known for twelve years. Jeremy hired him to insulate houses at $18.00/hour. The owner checked his record, and the state would not allow him to take the job because he had been incarcerated. Then, I found him another job at Randstad, another company, and Shane went for his interview, and they gave him his card to start. Shane, a day later, got a call and said they could not hire him for the same reasons as his record. I, as a mother, was very upset about this. I felt this was wrong because he was never arrested for any violent crime. Shane was very depressed because of this. He was trying to get his license back trying to pay child support, and the justice system failed him. Shane decided to go back to roofing. That's all he knew how to do. Most addicts that couldn't find jobs did roofing because most roofers would hire them. From the age of fifteen, Shane learned roofing from his stepfather Ray.

Shane started dating a girl named Laura. She seemed to me a good girl. She drove him back and forth to work and took him to the gym.

She was a good person, but my son, missing his boy, decided to leave her and wanted to try to make it with his son's mom. I felt bad for her when they parted. I felt at this time my son had already relapsed, which Laura had hinted to me. They were not together much longer than maybe two months. Today she is married with a little girl, and I am so happy for her. It was around October 2011 that Shane ended up going back with the mother of his son.

It was the beginning of November 2011; while Shane was living with his son, Jeannette had left her new baby's father. Shane was happy to be home with his son. He read to him every night. Shane was also good to her new daughter. The mother got tired of driving him to work every morning because Shane lost his license because of his bad choices. Jeannette had to work and had the baby and his son Cody. She also believed my son was using it again. That was in late January 2012. Things didn't last long. One of the workers at the roofing company gave Shane Vicodin, which made him go back to heroin.

Shane had visitation at first, with his son seeing him every other weekend. Jeanette started making it hard for his visitation with his son because Shane started dating a girl that was using drugs. In the meantime, Jeannette went back to her baby's father. Shane's new girlfriend. I despised her. She was just as much of a heroin addict as he was. I started looking for help to find a place. I wanted to be able to take his son for nights so his son Cody would have his own room. I found a trailer in Peabody for Shane to move to where his son could stay when he visited. This was a two-bedroom trailer, and it needed a bit of work, like the kitchen floor, which the floor tiles needed to replace. Shane fixed up the floor and also built shelves. He made that deal with the landlord. The girlfriend ended up moving all her stuff in and took over his son Cody's room with her computer stuff. I was so mad with this girl, for she knew he had a son but lost visitation with her own. Jeannette gave me permission to supervise the visits with my son Shane and his son Cody because Jeanette didn't want Shane's girl around their child. The supervised visits didn't last too long. I packed up the lunches and was looking forward to having his son spend the day with his dad. When I arrived at my son's home, my son walked to my car and sat in the back seat with his son. Shane was high that day. I took Cody to York Maine Zoo in the past. He loved feeding the animals and going on kid rides. I started to talk to Shane. His words were slurring, and his eyes were bright, glassy blue. He told me he did not want to drive all the way to that zoo. He was high on heroin. I then told him to get out of the car now. He disgusted me. Cody was looking forward to it. I felt so bad for my grandson. He wasn't four years old yet. I did not want my grandson to see his dad like that. Cody and I went to the zoo alone. Jeanette started making things difficult for my son and was upset about what my son did. I could not blame her for not wanting her son around what they both were doing. Cody's mom had taken me off supervised visits. She gave me an ultimatum: I stop court supervision, or I will not see Cody. She was right about the stuff my son was doing with that girl, and I was in the middle and wanted my grandson in my life. Her boyfriend at that time made it difficult because he was jealous of my son, which made it even harder on both myself and Shane. They were then married, and today they are divorced. During their marriage, Cody would call him daddy, which hurt my son.

Shane went back to the Methadone clinic, but he was still using heroin. They would use Methadone to feel better until they could get more heroin. This was upsetting to me and his son's mom. She had Shane have hair follicle testing done by the court, which showed he tested positive. The Court gave Shane supervised visits with his son with a court-appointed supervisor, which cost eighty dollars for two hours. There were a few times I directly paid a court-appointed supervisor. It was hard for Shane because he had to pay rent, utilities, child support, and visits. Shane was allowed to talk to his son at seven pm every night. Sometimes, Jeanette made it hard because of her girlfriend. Everybody warned him about her, but he didn't listen. Hanging out with someone else doing drugs is not a good thing. The new girlfriend introduced Shane to new people. Shane was getting worse and using more drugs. Both were not in a good place.

Shane Called Out for Help

Shane called me crying to help him, "Mom, I can't do this chasing drugs anymore."

Shane wanted to stay clean, but we all know that drugs take over the brain. He was running the streets sleeping here and there. Shane now tries the Suboxone clinic. He waited from January 2012 almost three months to see his doctor get a prescription. He had to see a counselor first for a couple of months; then, it wouldn't have been until April 2012 to get the Suboxone. While waiting to get to see the doctor, Shane was set up by his friend with drugs. Two months later, in March, it was the gun.

Shane did not start the Suboxone clinic until April. A friend of a known acquaintance asked if my son would get him a bag of cocaine and that he would drive him to that friend. This was taking place at the Beverly Cummings Center, and my son had no idea that the person he met was an undercover police officer. Shane was not arrested for that. They waited so they could make a bigger bust. Then another known friend set him up selling the gun, which took place at the Shaws' plaza in Beverly. All present were his drug buddies, and the gun did not belong to him, but money was all he cared about for him feeding his drug habit. That's how long it took to see his doctor. Shane shouldn't have had to wait to get to the clinic. He should have been getting the help he needed. The system failed him. Shane was arrested at his trailer in Peabody. During those nineteen months, Shane didn't know he was being indicted for the drug and gun charge. The Suboxone doctor recommended he go back to the Methadone clinic because Suboxone wasn't helping him. While he was at the Methadone Clinic, Shane signed a release form for me so I would know if he failed a drug test. Here are the letters that I gave to his federal lawyer for his defense in court to prove that he was trying to do everything he could to stay clean.

The Big Arrest That Tore My Heart

Shane finally started doing well. Doing the Methadone treatment was beginning to help. Then the arrest came in July 2013. The cops were there with guns, and they used a Taser on him because he wouldn't kneel in the broken glass from the window they broke. The Peabody officer asked him, "Do you remember what you were arrested for?"

Shane answered, "No!"

"The gun, Shane."

Shane replied, "OH FUCK!"

When I got the phone call that he was arrested, I was sick to my stomach. I felt that if he got to see the doctor earlier, he would have received the help he needed. In my eyes, I felt it was entrapment because they used my son's acquaintance, who had a longer rap sheet than Shane. The acquaintance helped the marshals set him up. It was the same kid who set my kid up, having my son sell him drugs two months prior. That was twice the kid set my son up. Shane did it because he owed him $400. That acquaintance called and called my son until he agreed to do it. Shane and I shared the same phone plan, so I gave his federal lawyer copies of the phone bill, and they showed the phone calls that were made by the person that was setting him up. The other person who owned the gun that was present was also set up. That was Shane's co-defendant, and he received twenty-four months in prison because he didn't have any serious priors. Shane was indicted in 2013. The Federal Court charged him with two indictments, the drugs and the gun. Shane pleaded out for ten years instead of getting fifteen. While he was being sentenced, the judge asked him if he had anything to say.

Shane replied, "First, I want to thank your honor for the opportunity to speak. I would like to take this opportunity to express to the Court how apologetic I am not only to my family but to the community as a whole. Now that I am sober, I can reflect on how my decisions affected both the community and my family. Not only do I feel ashamed of what I did, but I also feel humiliated. Reflecting on the hoices I made, I now know they were wrong. If given the choice again, I assure you they would be different. Not because I was caught but because I am sober. The time I am going to be incarcerated will not be wasted. I will utilize the time wisely fighting my addiction and coming out as a pro-social member of my community. That is a promise. Through the drug program and any other programs at my disposal, I plan on fighting my addiction. I will work on bettering myself and not come out with the same person I went in with that I promised to my family and community. Again, thanks for allowing me the opportunity to address the Court."

My letter to the Honorable Judge Young before Shane was sentenced:

Dear Honorable Judge Young,

As you know, it has been a crisis in our country in the world of drugs. Our doctors put the drug Oxycodone from their hands into the streets of our children. Governor Patrick has declared a state of emergency on opiate abuse. I wish they had done that twelve years ago. My son Shane has been a victim of this drug since 2002. Then he became hooked on heroin because it was cheaper on the streets. Shane almost died on November 3, 2004, the same year. His life was saved thanks to a police officer who gave him Narcan, a drug that reverses the effect. The drug, your Honor, as you know, takes over the receptors of the brain, and there is still no real cure. Putting Shane on a substitute drug which is still a drug and a high, cannot fix the problem. My son had waited months for treatment each time, in which you had to be high to get into the program. He has put himself through drug court, where if you had relapsed and failed the drug screen, you were sent to jail for three weeks, which Shane was. I had written many letters over the years to John Tierney's office, which his lawyer has copies of, and I asked to get the best treatment centers for us parents could afford. I had a vigil in 2006 in which I read 200 names of young and old that had died from this terrible drug. I just recently wrote a letter to the editor to stop the FDA from releasing the new opiate Zohydro ER, WHICH WE

MORE DEADLY. I wrote to and called government officials with my opinion. I was happy to hear that Governor Patrick banned that drug in Massachusetts. The Supreme Court overturned his decision, which I was not happy with. Also, I feel that incarcerating individuals like my son save their lives at the time, but there have never been intense treatments in the prisons to just do that. Coming home after being incarcerated, my son cannot find a job or afford to get an apartment and take care of his obligations to his son, so they get depressed and relapse, and that is what brings them right back here for our system that fails them. So, I am hoping he can get some schooling in. My son never hurt anyone but himself. Shane has always struggled with his addiction and always came to me for help. I am not making any excuses for what he did, but it was not my son who did it. It was his sickness, a disease. My son wants help if there is help out there, and he wants to return to society with a good job. He wants to be a good father when he comes home to his son Cody, who will be seven this January. My son was waiting for treatment when he committed this crime and was in treatment when they arrested him nineteen months later. I only hope someday; they can work on a cure for opiate addiction. I feel it is like any other disease. I am a mother who loves her son and who will continue fighting the war on drugs. Hopefully, we will save our grandchildren from making the same mistakes.

Thank you,

A grieving mother,

Denise Hansen

There was a burst of tears pouring down my cheeks. I could not believe an addict who is a sick person would get sentenced to ten years. Shane was a non-violent twenty-seven-year-old kid. Rachael lost her only brother and sibling. He lost his good friend Danny and his girl, who also sat in the courtroom with us. I did not believe what they heard from this judge. Shane had to wait four months to go in front of Judge O'Toole because he was working on the case of the Boston bomber.

This was for the drug case. At the end of four months, Shane went in front of Judge O'Toole for the drug charge, and he ran it concurrently with the gun charge that Judge Young gave him. I was very upset because murderers and rapists don't get this. Shane is not a violent offender. He never hurt anyone but himself. Shane is a drug addict. I don't believe in using other junkies' friends to set up other people. I think it should be illegal. I feel it's entrapment. I was hoping it would have been less. As the marshals led him out of the Court House, they would not let me hug him goodbye. I felt this was so cruel to do to him. Shane had already set in his mind that he was getting ten years; he had plenty of time to have it sink in. Plead out to ten years instead of fifteen. This was not justice. I kept fighting by writing letters and calling Congress for changes.

The following is an article I put in the Salem News:

They Should Have Never Legalized Syringes

"The opioid problem is serious, especially with the fentanyl that is being mixed in heroin. Narcan is also being used so much that people are overdosing over and over again and becoming immune to the drug. The police, fire department, or whoever has to administer this drug two to three times, and most times, it will not bring them back.

I have been through this for thirteen years with my son, and I am not blind to these drugs. The syringes should have never been legalized in 2007. Unauthorized use of a syringe should be illegal, with time served for possession of a needle. (SEE PG 103)

These kids are walking into a Walgreens at eighteen years old and buying them, so they shoot the drug into their veins. You are allowing this to happen. These users are not stupid about AIDS and Hepatitis C. They clean them, believe me. These users know better not to share a needle. They have learned this and have known about it for years.

You cannot cure a person who dies from an overdose. Look at the average of deaths before 2007 compared to now. It's outrageous. The government has to put a stop to these needles now. They are being found by young children all over the streets and beaches. It is disgusting.

As a mother of a heroin addict and knowing the struggles of his addiction, I think the problem would be far less a problem if you remove the legalization of syringes. The Suboxone strips are getting into our prison systems. Maybe they should give them out by a doctor for heroin users instead so they don't abuse it to get high. That is the only drug I approve of until they finally reach out for a cure. They can make all these drugs that harm our bodies but work on nothing to fix it.

Also, I would like to say the justice system has to be dealt with. People who commit worse crimes, like manslaughter or rape, get nothing. What about the sick addicts who never hurt anyone but themselves who get ten to fifteen years? The system is not working, e.g., One of my son's good friends, Mark De Voe, was in a road rage in Lowell, Massachusetts. Mark DeVoe was shot in the chest on February 15, 2018. A twenty-one-year-old woman, Garcia Palino, bragged about it on Facebook how she shot him. In court, she admitted she shot him, and she got 9 ½ years for murder. His parents were devastated. His father, Ron DeVoe, spoke on national tv and said, "The justice system stinks." Another example just recently, a twenty-three-year-old man from Lawrence was found guilty of child rape and other assault charges. He was sentenced to seven to nine years. With good time, he'll get out at six. She should have gotten a life sentence. I can go on and on, but I want to say this Justice system is not working. It's not fair. There is no justice. My son never hurt a soul in his life, and look at what he got."

These past fifteen years of my life have been lonely, the most costly, and more tears because of my son's addiction. I don't get to see my grandson. It has been five years since I've seen him. He is now twelve. If my son had gotten help during those years and with all the hard work I've done with letters and drug awareness, he would be home with me and not over five hundred miles away. It's now seven years later, and Shane is 1447 miles from home. We understand most of the politicians do not have a clue or have been through Hell themselves with a loved one. I know; I have their returned letters. No addict deserves to be isolated. We need everyone to get on board. We need better long-term facilities. If they can build new homes, roads, and factories, why can't we build a big home in every state for our children to get clean and get the help they need? STOP incarceration for non-violent drug offenders in the state and federal systems. Addicts should not be punished; they are sick. I am asking the State and Congress to fight for all children, to give them hope so they can live a long, productive life and receive the therapy they need. Every one of us has made the wrong choice in our lifetime. We need to stop and think about how an addict feels, how they know they made a bad choice and tried but could not control it. Syringes and the injection sites are all a form of enabling."

The suffering of an addict as the drug affects their brain is so intense and so very sad. My son is alive and spending ten years in federal prison for a disease he could not control. If needles were not legalized in 2007, I believe the death toll would have been different today.

I always asked my son's lawyer to put him in rehabilitation instead of three years in jail. I don't believe a heroin addict dealer who, in need of a fix, sells a little here and there should get a life sentence. The higher-ups that bring in tons of this drug should get a life sentence. There are way too many drug dealers who do not even touch the drug; they just sell it. They should not blame the addicts. It is explained in black and white that heroin takes over the brain.

I also want to say the federal guidelines should decrease the time in prison for drug addicts or let them be put in a place where they are constantly getting the help they need. My son was sent to a maximum-security prison, which most people there are doing. Shane's crimes were all caused by his addiction, and he never hurt anyone in his life but himself. Why do they put addicts in a place like that? It is crazy and unfair. People are getting stabbed every day; an addict should not have to be put in a position like that. Some murderers aren't sentenced to ten years, but a sick person is.

The loss of family is something I have to live with every day. I lost visitation with my grandson, not because I was bad, but because my son became a heroin addict. The loss of him is overbearing, and the courts don't care if they take the family away from the people they love. The fact is a father should have the right to be able to have contact with his son, especially if he never harmed them in any way. Heroin is a bad disease, and it hurts everyone involved.

Talking to an inmate on the phone costs three dollars a call, but if you use a phone company, you get charged extra. It costs taxpayers way more to put someone in prison than rehab. The parent has to do the time for his crime, which is utterly wrong. If they know what opioids do to the brain from all the painkillers they put on our streets, then why can't they come up with a cure? I read that the Sackler family has built a fourteen billion dollar fortune selling Oxycontin. The drug kills more people and it is FDA-approved. With all their money, why can't they compensate the families that lost their children because of Oxycodone? Last, I would like to say Narcan is a great thing, and it saved a lot of lives, but only for the moment. Most of the users end up overdosing the next day. We need to clean up the federal guidelines and state prisons for addicts and find a cure."

In early 2015 I wrote an article for Salem News. It was called

"Jail Always Seemed the Better Answer"

"I am writing this letter because I want to let everyone know about heroin addiction and what they never did to help my son. As you said in the article about my son ("Shane Hansen of Peabody gets ten years in the gun, heroin cases.," April 13), having his addiction way back when he overdosed on Nov 3, 2004, my son was nineteen years old. In June, he will be thirty.

The responses I showed you from Congressman John Tierney. I wrote many letters to congressmen, senators and Charlie Baker's office, and Maura Healey's office. All I ever got was they were working on it, and they were trying their best they could to fight this epidemic.

It has been nine years since the vigil I had at the Peabody Common. My son was serving a year for possession and dirty urine when he put himself in the Drug Court in Lynn.

I begged the judge to put him in rehab somewhere, but jail always seemed the better answer for everyone. He did not like me at all. There were no beds back then, and there are still no beds. They have rehabbed all over, but one has to be on a list and wait. How do you tell a sick person with a disease he or she has to wait? When a child is sick, does the parent who loves them have to wait to see the doctor? That is how it is today and has been for eleven years. My son tried to stay clean many times with Methadone and Suboxone.

Those drugs are pacifiers to the receptors of their brain, and if you stop pacifying them, they want that drug again. My son chose to do Oxycodone as a lot of other kids did. They did not know this opioid would take over their brains and torch them. I mean, if they could not satisfy the receptor, it would make them sick. I have witnessed my son being sick, and it is not a pretty picture. We all know most of them turned to shooting heroin. They commit crimes, and they go to jail. They get called junkies by the officials, and some brutally abuse them. I have experienced it and see more of it on the news.

These police officers out there should be helping the kids get well, not using them or abusing them. My son Shane was used to it. They set him up with an informant. Somehow, he knew. Why didn't they help him instead? Most addicts sell to make money to take care of their sick habits. You need to be high to get into the Methadone and Suboxone program, or they will not take you. You would think that his history would speak for itself. Shane's record is all due to his addiction to heroin. If they built a facility like Middleton and had it just for intense rehab and it was affordable, my son would not be serving ten years, nor would he have sold a gun. Never before did he sell a gun before or after that one time in 2012.

In August 2016, I decided to organize an opioid addiction walk. I ordered shirts that read "HELP FIGHT OPIOID ADDICTION." It was held at the Peabody Commons in Peabody, Massachusetts. The people that attended were State Representative Joan Lovely, Anne Meeker from Seth Moulton's Office., and Peabody Police. I got help with the raffle table from my daughter Rachel, Kelly Quirk, and Maureen Ouellette, and all the support from my family and friends.

I'd like to thank everyone for being here. It means the world to me. Not only for my son but for everyone's child is everyone's epidemic.

I stood here almost fourteen years ago with my friend Maureen Oulette. We organized a vigil and awareness together. We were asking for better treatment, more beds, and rehabilitation instead of prison. There hasn't been anything accomplished in all this time. There have been more overdoses in the last thirteen years than in the 70s. The legalization of syringes only enabled addicts and caused overdoses to skyrocket since 2007. The injection sites they want to put in are insane. That will enable all who were struggling to stay clean. Giving drug dealers the right to sell their drugs is against the wall. Why not put in Vivitrol shot sites? That drug does not contain any opiates. It will save the taxpayers money having a drug available with no opiates. Drug dealers will lose.

I wanted to organize this walk for the sake of everyone, their children, their grandchildren, and all of you who lost a loved one.

I sat in my living room one day, and I made a few phone calls. I called Mass General and Harvard University. I got other phone numbers from them. I was trying to find a lab that was actually working on something to replace Suboxone and Methadone (which is an opiate that acts as a pacifier until you stop).

Methadone is very bad for your body. It's harder to withdraw from. Suboxone is getting into our prisons, and it's being sold to get high. How do I know? It's from experience with my son, who's been serving for ten years. He never hurt anyone but himself. He never had any rehab. He never had any help. He's just been doing a hard time.

This is no life for anyone and not for the parents who suffer. By making numerous phone calls, I finally found a place called the University of Texas Medical Branch Addiction Research Center. They are a medical branch working in a lab fighting these using experiments on mice to figure out why the brain is addicted to Cocaine and Heroin. They are trying to find something other than using opiates. They want to help and give it to all who are addicted. They are working very hard. Ph.D. Dr. Catherine Cunningham sent me her resources. You can grab one and read about what they're doing. It's far better than waiting another fourteen years with no accomplishments. They are working with me in this fight, and I am overwhelmed with what they want to accomplish.

So, please, all donations are appreciated. Please listen to the speakers, and enjoy the music and refreshments. I'd like to thank the band Second Time Around for donating their time. I want to thank Bob Rapeoza, who'll be speaking, and Ron Doe. I also want to thank Paul Malphy. I need all of you to hear from Marc Mero, a recovered addict. It was too much to get him here, so I brought his DVD. I also want to thank two of my good friends who lost their children to drugs. I want to thank Mary Ellen Miller and Maureen Ouellette. Thank you, everyone, for coming. If any representatives are here, you may speak at 2:30 if you like. Also, thank you to the Porta Potty guy.

Approximately ninety people showed up. I raised $2338.00. The money went to the University of Texas Medical Branch Research Center. They're a medical branch trying to develop a cure for addiction and why the brain addicts to heroin and other addicting stuff. They're trying to find something other than opiates. The lady I worked with that helped me at the branch was Dr. Kathryn Cunningham, Ph.D. She sent me all the resources to share.

My friend Maureen spoke about losing her son Brandon. "My name is Maureen Ouellette. I am here today to share my story about my son Brandon who passed away in 2011. He was only twenty-six. Brandon died from a Pulmonary Embolism, which was caused by IV use. It damaged the heart, and doctors were not able to keep his heart

49

going. He started using Oxycontin in high school and then switched to Heroin because it was cheaper. Brandon went to a holding facility in Tewksbury. There were never any beds, and then I had sectioned him to Bridgewater. Brandon got clean for a while and then relapsed. My son was a caring, loving, funny person. Everyone that knew him loved him. Methadone never helped. I, as a mom, tried all I could do to help my son. He wanted the help, but he was so addicted, and he told me how badly he wanted it. No one can understand this is a disease. The pain in my heart and my memories of my son will always be here with me. He was and always will be my angel."

Below is a copy of the letter I received from the President of UMB Health:

October 10, 2017
79 Rantoul Street, Apt 315
Beverly, MA, 01915
Dear Mrs. Hansen,
We're grateful for your recent contribution to support the UTMB Center for Addiction Research. Through your generosity, we can recognize outstanding faculty who are conducting pioneering investigations, particularly in the area of opioid addiction.
Thank you for graciously contributing to UTMB's biomedical research mission. We appreciate you partnering with us as we strive to control the grip of addiction on people, giving hope to millions around the world.
Sincerely,
David L. Calendar, MD, MBA, FACS
President

I also received a letter from Seth Moulton's Office about organizing the walk. Here is the letter:

Massachusetts
September 6, 2017
Dear Denise,
Thank you for your hard work and dedication in organizing the 1st
Annual Walk to Conquer Opiate Addiction in Peabody. I heard from
my staffer, Anne, that it was a beautiful and deeply moving event. Your
advocacy on behalf of your son and all families affected by the opiate
crisis is inspiring to us all.
My casework team and I will keep fighting for your son's treatment
and for a fairer, more effective justice and addiction treatment system
for all Americans.
Best,
SETH MOULTON
Member of Congress

On October 21, 2017, I spoke at a forum at the Quincy Kennedy
Library. I met the people that had this forum at the State House in
Boston, and they invited me to come speak. We were there to speak
against injection sites. There were some parents who lost their sons or
daughters who thought injection sites were good, and some who
wanted their kids to go to them.

I am totally against injection sites because it does not help them.
Treatment helps them. Keeping putting heroin in someone's body does
not cure them; it poisons them. Treatment is what I've been fighting for
years. I met great people at the State House, the ones that were there
against the injection sites.

I READ MY LETTER AT THE HEARING OF MENTAL
HEALTH SUBSTANCE USE AND RECOVERY AND AT THE
STATE HOUSE IN BOSTON, MA.

Regarding the bill on injection sites S1081

I am a mother of a heroin addict; my son Shane is serving ten years in federal prison, not for hurting anyone or does he have violent crime, but was charged with one in the federal court, and I do not believe in anyone with a disease should be sentenced so harshly. Shane has a disease like thousands of our children, and yes, thousands have died, but the solution is not enabling them just like they did in 2007 by legalizing syringes which made the epidemic skyrocket since. With injection sites, you're allowing drug dealers to continue selling drugs in which heroin is illegal and poisons their bodies. Heroin destroys their teeth and every organ in their body, and nowadays, it is not heroin; it is pure Fentanyl. Some people like my son, who had a $250 dollar habit a day, and bet some have more. Does anyone honestly think when they leave an injection site that, addicts will run, travel back, or whatever to get their next fix? They will go back to their dealer, whoever it may be, to get more and may not make it back. Addicts do not care; they do not think like that. What about the ones that were clean, and their parents paid big bucks to send them to a good treatment facility out of state? Maybe that could trigger them to say oh, I can go to this site now and get high, and I might not die. Heroin takes over their brain receptors, and you're an addict for the rest of your life; easy to relapse, especially if it is right in front of you. My son comes home and knows that these sites could be tempting, and this worries me. Why is there no chemist or scientist working on finding a cure? Instead of lining them up at methadone clinics and getting suboxone which still has opiates in them, and plus, there find needles everywhere. I have been advocating for my son and other addicts since 2003, and from my experience, I know and have lived it. I know what drugs do to them. I will be damned if they allow these Facilities. No chemical with opiate in it, which I believe can help an addict. The absence of opiates in their receptor is the only way to treatment. Unless you are a family member, a mom, dad, sister, brother, wife, or husband, you will not

nderstand the pain that we endure. I will keep fighting my way, and
his way is not enabling.

Shane Starts His Sentence In the BOP

Shane was sent to Plymouth County Correctional Facility in Mass-
chusetts, where he spent over a year. Plymouth held federal prisoners
s well as state offenders. I visited Shane many times while he was
vaiting to be sentenced at the Federal Courthouse in Boston.

Shane's cousin Lee passed away on December 8, 2013, from a car
ccident while Shane was incarcerated. Shane took this very hard. The
wo of them were very close. I had given my son the news that he
tarted to cry. He cried loudly, and I could hear in his voice the pain he
vas going through and how it hurt he could not be home for his family.

Shane never caused any problems back in Plymouth. I started
vorking with his federally-appointed lawyer. I was home working on
iis charges for two small possessions of heroin. One was in Lynn,
Massachusetts, and the other one was in Salem District Court. I had to
get him an appointed state lawyer to dismiss Shane's cases of the
harges of heroin that were tested by the lab in 1997 by Annie
Dookhan (convicted felon who worked as a chemist at the Mass-
chusetts Department of Public Health Drug of Abuse Lab and admit-
ing to falsifying evidence affecting 34,000 cases).

I worked very hard on those two cases to be dismissed and made
ure there were no others so that when my son was sentenced, they
vouldn't be used against him. I succeeded after waiting a year to
emove them from his record. For the case of assault on a Peabody
Police Officer, I hired another free defense lawyer who knew my son
rom his previous lawyer, who now is a judge. Shane swore he never
aused him to fall and that he fell over his own two feet. Shane turned
eventeen at the time of the charge. The police officer had a report that
ie got checked out of the Lahey Clinic for a scraped arm, so I could
iot get that dismissed. The assault was dropped on his record, but the
langerous weapon (a bicycle) was not. This hurt my son in his

sentences, even though he just turned seventeen. I worked so hard fighting for my son.

Shane had to go before two judges at the Federal John Moakley Courthouse in Boston, Massachusetts. Back then, I could not understand why both charges were not with one judge. Judge Young was one of the toughest and sentenced Shane to ten years on possession of a firearm under USC18 922 j in January 2015. Shane had to wait until April of 2015 for the drug charge in front of Judge O'Toole, who ran his sentence currently with Judge Young's sentence. Judge O'Toole was working on the bomber case at the time. Later in 2017, when Shane was in Hazleton, Shane found on his computation paper that he did not credit for four months waiting for Judge O'Toole's sentence. I called his federal lawyer to file a motion for Judge O'Toole to get back his four months. It took a year to comply.

After the long wait at Plymouth County, Shane was sent to Brooklyn MDC, where all his tattoos were checked out to see if he was a gang member. They were also looking at his record and point system to see where he was going to serve his ten years.

Canaan USP High Max Penitentiary

Canaan was located in Waymart, Pennsylvania. Neither Shane nor I could figure out why he was sent to a USP High max. My son's letters to me talk about how much he misses his son and how he cannot talk to him because the judge would not allow it. This hurt me as much as it hurt him. My son was not charged with a violent crime in federal court, and both judges recommended he do the 500 RDAP Drug Program. His federal lawyer promised me he would not go to a penitentiary, but he did. I was so upset with the system because this was wrong. He never murdered anyone or got caught with tons of drugs or guns. He only hurt himself, being a heroin addict feeding himself so he wouldn't be sick. During Shane's time in that Federal Penn, which was only a year at this prison, he complained about the food, just sandwiches every day. Shane also talked about how high it was up in the mountains. He said the watchtowers are up in the clouds, and it looks like mountains covered in snow and raining a lot there. They call it "Raining Canaan." Shane was accused of selling drugs through the mail. There were four guys; two of them were guilty, and the other two were innocent. Shane was one of the innocents. Shane was sent to the SHU known as the hole, where he spent ninety days. Shane ripped a face cloth in half while in the hole and cleaned the dirty bed. He told me there was hair all over it, and it was dirty. They were only given a clean face cloth three times a week. Shane was charged with destruction of property. I laughed about that because the taxpayers pay for the property, not the staff. Shane lost eight days of a good time. In another incident, Shane allowed an inmate to use his phone and lost time for that too. Spending ninety days in the hole before someone is found guilty is wrong. The law is that everyone is innocent until proven guilty. Shane didn't understand them moving him since he was innocent, but he was moved anyway. Now, after finding my son innocent, they move him to Allenwood, PA.

Allenwood USP Penitentiary

From the hole in Canaan, Shane was sent to Allenwood USP Penitentiary in Pennsylvania. Known as a better Penn, Shane spent a year there. He was trying to do the right thing and get his GED, but everyone knows what can happen when you meet other people like himself or worse.

Shane had a $250/day heroin addiction when he was home. Relapse is part of the recovery. Back then, I was fighting for his Hep C treatment. Shane signed a release form with his doctor at Allenwood that permitted me to talk to him. He also signed a form with Congressman Seth Moulton's Office in Massachusetts. They were going to start Shane on his Hep C treatment. Shane ended up with dirty urine for Suboxone. Suboxone is a drug that helps addicts keep themselves from doing heroin. I never said my son didn't make bad choices; he did. Addiction is a hard and tough disease to overcome. I was so upset because they did not give him his Hep C treatment. They always made excuses. Shane already had HEP C for ten years, and he would die in prison waiting for his long sentence to be over. Suboxone does not affect the liver. The health department for the BOP and the doctor from Allenwood told me that you had to be a level one or two. In their words, they already had to be sick. This made me furious, and I wanted to fight harder. I was so upset I asked his counselor if they could send him somewhere to get help. I argued with his prison counselor about his addiction. The counselor was so mean. His councilor's exact words were, "We're going to send him far away." The guy was a prick. This time my son did not know where he was going and hoped it was not like Canaan. After he was in the hole for ninety days for relapsing, they took two years of his visits away. One year's visit would have been behind glass. I wouldn't have traveled all that way for an hour's visit. Ninety days in the hole, which is a cement room as big as a parking lot, segregation. Then they sent him to a much worse prison, USP Hazelton (Misery Mountain), 587 miles from home. I never understood why he went to Penn in the first place or didn't go to a place where he could get the RDAP Program which was on his judgment. They had that program at Allenwood where he should have given him the help he needed there. My son needed help. Addicts cannot control their habits. Keeping someone locked up and confined does not help the situation. Productivity does, and treating them like human beings with dignity will. I wrote letters to Seth Moulton's office telling them my son needs treatment even though Suboxone does not affect the liver. This counselor was a real dink, to have to say. Addicts should be treated like a person with any disease. Punishing them is sickening to me. This prison was supposed to be one of the best around and closer to my home in Massachusetts. My thoughts are if a person relapses, should they punish them? This is the great BOP system.

Three years in Hazelton USP Penitentiary

Shane's time in Hazelton in 2017 was horrifying to me. I called the Bureau of Prisons in Grand Prairie, Texas, and spoke to a designated person. I asked him why Shane went to a penitentiary in the first place. I have no idea why I waited so long to ask the question. the officer replied back to me and said, "It was because Shane had an open case."

I replied, "No way does he have an open case." My son never had an open case. The lawyer should have known this before sentencing. His lawyer told me after leaving the federal courthouse in Boston, after sentencing, that Shane would never go to a penitentiary for a non-violent crime. I was told to go to the Salem District Court in Massachusetts and look the case up which the woman I spoke to at Salem. The woman replied, "It had been closed since 2008, and it was their error." The woman in Salem sent a copy of it to the Bureau of Prisons. She also sent a copy to the Administration Office in Hazleton. That removed three points from his points system.

An inmate was given points going on the severity of their record. An inmate who would have had sixteen points would go to a minimum, and twenty-three points would go to medium security and anything above high max security. Shane and I thought it would have been a medium on his record. This mistake should have been caught before he was sentenced in the first place. My son should have gone to a medium, not a high max. Hazelton had to have been the worst place for any non-violent addict to have been sent. They were treated like animals surrounded by lifers, rapists, and worse criminals and, most of all, more drugs.

Shane tried hard to get his GED and worked as a barber, which he was great at. He was hoping to do this in the future when he's released. I am a cosmetologist myself so he must have inherited his talent from me. The place was always locked down on holidays and long weekends, and there was no talking to families, which was non-stop lockdowns. The whole prison was locked down when there were stabbings or fights, all because of one person.

Then I continued fighting for his HEP C treatment. Shane would die in prison without treatment. I wrote letters to Congressmen Markey, Moulton, and Elizabeth Warren's Office. I worked mostly with Seth Moulton's office. Their offices sent me copies of the responses from the Department of Justice.

Going forward in my story, you will see copies of letters I received from Congress that they received from Hazelton saying that my son didn't need the treatment. I kept arguing with the Congressman that my son did need the treatment and he would have died without it. None of these Congressmen gave a damn about them or anyone. All the fighting I did, they did nothing. Seth Moulton's office did more than any other Congressman in Massachusetts. They seemed to have given up after they found out about his relapse.

The following is a response from Markey's Office:
August 23, 2017

Mr. Edward J Markey
United States Senator
975 JFK Federal Building
15 New Sudbury Street
Boston, Massachusetts, 02201
ATTN: Tristan Takos

Dear Senator Markey:

This is in response to your correspondence dated July 14, 2017, in reference to Shane Hansen, Register Number 95415-038, an inmate housed at the United States Penitentiary (USP) Hazelton, Bruceton Mills, West Virginia.

Mr. Hansen arrived at USP Hazelton on March 17, 2017. He received an initial chronic care consultation on March 16, 2017, where he verbalized no complaints other than being tired from traveling. Mr. Hansen was informed that Health Services staff would monitor his loodwork in reference to his diagnosis of Hepatitis C. He referred him o the Psychology Department to begin drug and/or alcohol counseling.)n the same date, labs were completed, and it was determined that Mr. Iansen was not a candidate for treatment at that time due to his liver nzymes being only mildly elevated. He also did not present with any ther health conditions that would qualify him as a priority case for reatment.

On August 10, 2017, labs were repeated, and Mr. Hansen showed ontinued improvement in his liver enzyme levels. He now classifies as priority three and does not qualify for treatment. Health Services staff vill continue to monitor his labs, and if there is a decline in his status, request will be made to determine his eligibility for treatment, despite is history of drug use while in prison.

Mr. Hansen has not reported any further symptoms to the Health Services Department that would indicate he is having a decline in his vellness. Health Services last saw Mr. Hansen on May 24, 2017, with omplaints of an ingrown toenail. We have received no further corre-pondence from Mr. Hansen in regard to his treatment, and he has erbalized on numerous occasions his understanding of his plan of care. I trust this information will assist you. In the event you have urther questions or concerns, please feel free to contact me.

This is a copy of a letter I received from the House of Represen-atives:

October 23, 2017

Ms. Denise Hansen

79 Rantoul Street, Apt 315
Beverly, MA 01915

Dear Denise,

Please find enclosed the letter our office received from the Bureau of Prisons regarding Shane's treatment. Please don't hesitate to let me know if there is anything else I can do. I will keep you updated on our progress as we work with the BOP to change the standards for delaying treatment following a positive suboxone test, and let you know when we start organizing our opiate crisis hall early next year.

All my best to you and Shane, and please don't hesitate to let me know if there is anything else I can do for you.

Sincerely,

Anne Meeker

District Aide and Caseworker

Office of Congressman Seth Moulton (MA-06)

21 Front Street

Salem, MA, 01970

978-531-1669

The BOP told me Shane was fine, and the letters they sent to Congress about him relapsing on a Suboxone, which does not affect his liver, nor should it have held his treatment back. Liver levels are one, two, and three. The BOP kept saying to me that he was a level three and that they wait until he was a level one or two. This made me more determined to get my son the help he needed. I was not happy with the Massachusetts Congressman. They should have tried a little harder. No matter how many calls I made and how many trips I made to Seth Moulton's office, I decided to take it upon myself as I had done in the past.

There was no way Shane was only level three. He had this for ten years. If they had waited until he was a level one or two and had not been treated, it would have led to hepatitis, Cirrhosis, or liver cancer. I talked to his federal lawyer, and he gave me the name of another federal lawyer (Attorney Brian Kornbrath) in West Virginia. Attorney

Kornbrath wrote letters to the warden. I asked my son to get a copy of his medical records as soon as possible. I received them ASAP. I brought them down to Shane's liver doctor (Dr. Ingraham). The doctor looked them over and said my son needed the treatment ASAP.

This letter was sent to the West Virginia lawyer:

12/20/2017
Concerning:
Shane M Hansen
DOB 06/19/1985

To whom it may concern:
Mr. Hansen was under my care from 2000 to 2008 for chronic hepatitis C. Interferon therapy was deferred at that time. While Mr. Hansen has been incarcerated for some years, I have remained involved via communications with his mother, who advocates fiercely for him. She has provided me with copies of his BOP medical records for the last several years.
On reviewing the records, I see that he has the expected ongoing transaminase elevation indicative of continued chronic hepatitis C. I also see that he was approved for DAA therapy in 2016 but then tested positive for Suboxone. The record states that he was therefore disqualified for one year. However, one year has now passed, and I am hoping that he will be re-qualified for antiviral therapy.
Mr. Hansen now has a hepatitis C infection of more than one-decade standing and begins to enter a period of risk for the development of hepatic fibrosis and eventual cirrhosis. The community standard of care is to proceed with DAA therapy at this point. I hope, and recommend, that you provide this for him.
Sincerely,
Irving Ingraham MD

The West Virginia lawyer sent a copy of the doctor's letter to the warden in Hazleton. Shane was finally treated because he was not a level three. He was a level two. My son would never have finished a full sentence. He would have died in prison. I greatly appreciated the cooperation of Dr. Ingraham, M.D. He specializes in the liver. I was also thankful for Attorney Brian Kornbrath of West Virginia.

During my son's treatment, which was one dose daily, medical staff in prison skipped over my son's dose one morning because he was not up. For a reason, his toilet overflowed. Shane and his cellmate were up late, cleaning it up to early morning. The staff was supposed to try giving it to him that afternoon. Shane saw the doctor twice, but the staff refused to give it to him. His Liver treatment doses are not supposed to be missed. I emailed the doctor, and this was his answer to missing a dose.

3/12/2018
Concerning:
Shane M Hansen
176 Newbury St
Lot 8
Peabody MA 01960

To whom it may concern:
Mr. Hansen is undergoing treatment for hepatitis C with Harvoni. Hepatitis C is difficult to eradicate. It is important that Mr. Hansen does not miss a daily dose of Harvoni. If he misses taking it in the morning, he should take it later in the day.
Sincerely,
Irving Ingraham MD

Treatment is horrible in these prisons. They are supposed to treat them. They lied to me for almost two years and said he was a level three. The health department woman from the prison told me they wait until they are really sick at level one or two. That was their criteria. Shane would have been at the beginning stages of cirrhosis of the liver. The letter stated from Hazelton to Congress read that he did not complain about pain. The liver is silent. Thank God I went the route I had gone. (Please see all copies of Certificates of Achievement in the back of the book.)

This prison had so many lockdowns for months at a time. I cried myself to sleep, not hearing from my son. Just letters that sometimes took fifteen days to get. They were fed boxes of food, no hot meals, just cold sandwiches during the lockdown. There were times they had to bathe themselves from the sinks in the cell. I met many moms from the prisons and their brothers and sisters. We exchanged numbers so one would call the other to make sure our kids were safe. I am to this day in Groups of Facebook Families with Loved Ones Incarcerated. Their stories are heartbreaking. While my son was there in Hazleton, forty-eight-year-old Ian Thorne was killed during an altercation with a fellow prisoner. Demario Porter, twenty-seven, on a parole violation, was also killed in another fight with a fellow inmate. This is what makes it hard for families. These are things that cause so many lock-downs and segregation for months while they investigate. My thing is they have cameras. Why don't they use them instead of making everyone else suffer? Then, on October 30th, Whitely Bulger was found dead from a fatal beating at age eighty-nine. Whitey did not have many friends, but everyone questioned why a high profiler like him would be sent to an open population like that. The prison was in a twenty-four-hour lockdown for three months straight during the investigation. Inmates who should be proven guilty or innocent are put in solitary confinement to this day. This still remains in 2022. Nothing could be more depressing to all the inmates than being in a twenty=four hour lockdown. I could not visit my son. I was a mess knowing he wasn't getting any hot meals.

The lockdowns continued. The place was loaded with drugs, Suboxone, and K-2 marijuana. The inmates that took the K-2 mari-juana would flip-flop on the floor and hallucinate from it. Some inmates overdosed on it. In my opinion, I honestly believe that it's not just the visitors bringing in the drugs. Visitors are checked thoroughly when they go in. In my opinion, some guards bring the drugs in. Here in Massachusetts, two guards got probation for it (that's distribution). That should have been more than probation.

Shane was starting to get depressed not being able to see his son or me. We had done many Court dates by telephone conference, but my son never won a judgment. Missing his son was the worst for him because he was in his life when he left.

I saw my son once when he was in Canaan and twice while he was in Allenwood, both in Pennsylvania, approximately 547 miles from home. You wouldn't know whether there was a lockdown or not. It took me six and a half hours to drive there. The cost of the hotel, food, and gas was around $500.

Shane was offered to be sent to the USP Penitentiary in Beaumont, Texas, to take the RDAP Program. Shane refused because he had not seen me in two years. He wanted to wait until he got closer to home.

I wanted to see him so badly. Shane was allowed visits after two years. I took a trip to Hazelton and stayed in a hotel that was directly across from the prison, the Micro Inn Hotel. This was in nowhere land, and there was not a restaurant but some hillbilly place that looked scary and dark up around the corner. They just went on lockdown the night I arrived, and it was eleven hours to drive up and back. I was praying the next morning they would allow visits. I got a call from his cellmate's mom Jeannette who remains a good friend today, and said thank God they were out of lockdown. She was there to see her son also, but her ride was three hours or so. I got to see my son for the first time in two years. I had never hugged him so tight. Shane and I both cried. We had a great visit. I was allowed to get his food out of the vending machine, heat it in the microwave and put it in front of him, but we were not allowed to touch it again. Also, the visitors are checked thoroughly because of drug contraband. I stayed about five hours because they did count, and there was no moment for either one of us, so we would have to wait to leave. I also had my visit on Sunday.

Months passed by, and I missed my son. There have been too many lockdowns. That meant just getting letters. Shane would have een going to a medium level soon because his points had gone own.

Sometime in June of 2018, while Shane was in the chow hall, an inmate serving life asked him to beat up another inmate. Shane refused, nd the guy said the person owed him money.

Shane argued with the guy doing life, "That kid does not owe you money." This guy was not liked by anyone there. Shane refused his equest, and the inmate called my son a bitch in front of the other inmates. Shane took it upon himself to beat his ass, and he did just that. You cannot be a pussy in a prison-like that or any of them. Shane was ent to the hole for two days, and all the guys, blacks, whites, and Hispanics, went to the SIS (investigators) and told them they should let Shane out of the hole, and Shane was released back into the general population.

Shane was a barber there and cut everyone's hair. Many people liked him. That was his job there, but he was also trying to get his GED. He never got his GED because the lockdowns were almost every other week. So how is anyone going to better themselves in a place like that? Visits there were always canceled. They were eating like crap and could not go to the commissary. Everyone got punished for all others' bad behavior. Now, because of the fight, Shane lost some good time, and his points went up, and he never went to a medium facility. It was like they wanted him to fail.

Sometime towards the end of the year, Shane was charged with having drugs on a piece of a magazine on his sock. He was stripped down on his way to the chow hall. They accused my son of having three drugs in that magazine. They never sent it out to the lab to be tested. It is impossible to have three drugs in a piece of magazine. The magazine came from there. He was never sent any magazines. His story to me, which he always told me the truth after he was charged with, for example, the Suboxone, Shane told me while he was walking barefoot in his cell, using a can to sharpen his tool and then cutting up a magazine to test its sharpness for his barbering. When he put on his socks and shoes, a piece stuck to his sock. My son was drug tested at that time while he was in the hole. He was tested clean both times. My son said they did not send it out to a lab to be tested, so Shane appealed the charge, and it was denied. It took maybe two months for the appeal to come back. I remember it took a while. Shane wanted to appeal it a second time, but being in the hole, he had no contact with the cellmate who was going to help him. When the officer went by his cell, he would ask him about getting his paperwork so he could appeal again, but he would just be ignored. Shane got the shot which is disciplinary, at 8 pm and found it on his sock the next morning at 6 am. How does that make sense? The shot they call it comes after you find something and then charge him.

I have not seen my son for quite some time. I asked a friend to take a trip with me. We drove seven hours, reached Pennsylvania, and had to turn around. Shane would call me or email me to let me know if they were still out and not locked down, so I called to check to be sure, and they were. Gas and hotel money for the weekend was wasted. They never changed their answering machine, where you can call a number, and they tell you if there is a lockdown or not. I was so upset, crying all the way home, and they didn't give a shit. They don't care what it does to the families or how much we spend and how far we have to drive to see our loved ones. It is a crazy rule, and that is another thing that needs to be fixed. The BOP system is horrible and needs attention. Our families should not have to suffer. We should be able to see our children.

It was June 2019, and I planned to visit my son with a friend. The prison was in lockdown, so I waited until they just came off. I made my plans and stayed in a hotel in Morgantown which had a pool, restaurant, and everything right there, so much better. My friend stayed back at the hotel, and I had to drive just twenty minutes to the prison. I got to see my son Saturday and Sunday.

My last visit June 24, 2019.

Things were great during the visit. We laughed, we cried and talked about the old days and especially about his son Cody whom he missed so much. This is what puts my son in the depression he is in; all the lockdowns and hearing from the judgment from the Probate Family Court, he cannot talk to his son on the phone. My son has been in a state minimum prison; it was not as harsh and miserable. Federal is way worse, in my experience.

The visit ended on the second day. On Sunday, I went back to the hotel at noon. We had to drive eleven hours back. On the way home, I received a call from his cellmate Cody. He told me my son was sent right to the hole after my visit. I couldn't drive home. I was upset and crying. WHY? What happened now? The prison allowed me to see my son because they knew it was the last time. They knew he was not coming out for a long time, and I wouldn't see him. They normally would have put him in the SHU on Saturday. Shane relapsed, and he was tested for Suboxone. The prison was full of drugs, especially K-2 marijuana, which makes people hallucinate, and some people overdose, as I said. Shane told me that he relapsed, and it was because of being locked down so much and never could get a damn thing done and mostly the loss of contact with his son. He asked a CO (an officer at the prison) if he could do another drug program, and the CO said, "No, you did them all; we don't have anymore." That was upsetting to me because he could have repeated the same drug program. There were no other drug programs there.

Shane told me he struggled with it for a week. He kept saying to himself, 'Don't do it, don't do it.' I sent an e-mail to the administration in Hazelton and told them who the CO was who refused my son's help, and there was no response. I called his counselors and told them my son needed help, but they refused to give it to him. My son needs to go to the RDAP Program. It's on his judgment. His depression gets to him, and he needs to learn how to deal with it, but relapsing is part of recovery. During his time in the hole, he was still working on that second appeal for the drug on the magazine charge, but it never happened.

Shane has been in the hole twenty-three hours a day since June 24th waiting to find out where he was going to be sent. The administration wanted to send him to SMU, which is an administrative program in Illinois, 1447 miles from home. After he was charged with the drugs in the magazine, they wanted to send him to SMU at that time but decided not to. After this last Suboxone relapse, they decided they were sending him there. Relapse happens with addicts. It is a disease, something that a prisoner should be treated for and not punished.

For the next five months, the psychologist that was working with my son gave him packets of paperwork that helped him with his addiction. It was like homework for him.

The Hazelton Prison was in lockdown because of the flow of drugs. The whole segregation was full, and people were being sent to the medium facility right down the road, which had a camp and a medium facility on the same property. I argued with his counselor and called Seth Moulton's office to work with the BOP to get to a 500 RDAP program instead of sending him many miles away where they don't have any drug program. It seemed to be the problem with my son for many years, and it is still his addiction problem. Why not give him the help he needs? I argued this for five months while he sat in the hole.

He got certificates of completion for the packages he completed. (See pg. 103-104)

I know this might help my son, but I also believe in more treatment. Shane spent five months at Hazelton segregation complaining about no hot meals and getting just boxed meals like sandwiches. This is not healthy for anyone. Hazelton, to me, was like slavery. They are treated so inhumanely there. I believe that lifers should be in one prison and anyone with one to five years together and five to ten in another prison. This would cut down the stabbings and drug use. After five months of hell in Hazleton, they made up their mind to send my son to the SMU in Thomson, Illinois. I was so upset because he was still not getting any drug help, and he would be miles from home with no visits. Who knows what this will do to him being locked up twenty-three hours a day? I am glad he didn't take after me because I would have lost it for the first two days. The SMU used to be Lewisburg. The inmates were transferred to Thomson, and that facility is brand new and needs to be filled up. It holds fifteen hundred inmates. I read that some inmates at Lewisburg could not handle it and tried to cut their wrists. That is why they closed down the Lewisburg SMU. It became the most horrific facility in the federal prison. The prison cells were so small that two people in each cell could not move around. Lewisburg inmates soon learned forced proximity could, in its way, be just as torturous as extended solitary confinement. Sometimes close quarters can end up in violence. The transfer of inmates to the SMU In Thomson, Illinois, began late in 2018 and continued through 2019. The Thomson administration program is now well suited to house high-security inmates and other specialized missions for high-security inmates.

In November of 2019, Shane was moved to FCI in Hazelton but remained in segregation for two weeks until they flew him to Oklahoma City to be sent to Thomson. My son was accepted by the BOP to be sent to an RDAP program, and he was also accepted to the Administrative USP in Thomson, Illinois. To get letters from him, I would wait the whole day where I lived, and I could not do it anymore. The wait killed me every day. This is why I had to get USPS informed mail, where I would get an email early in the morning to show me if I had received a letter, and that would put me at rest. I would be happy if I saw one.

Shane Is Now In Smu In Illinois

Oklahoma City is a place where they transfer you from Illinois before they bus you to the next prison. I was very upset that my son was sent to the SMU instead of a facility closer to home and a drug program. I sent an email to the White House asking why my son and other addicts are not getting the help they need. Instead, they were sent to places like that and on a continuous twenty-three-hour lockdown.

About two weeks after Oklahoma, Shane was finally sent to the SMU (Special Management Unit). Shane was already in a twenty-three-hour lockdown for the past nine months. He said the food was better. He received three hot meals a day and even an apple or an orange with his breakfast and lunch. That is better where he was at Hazelton. He has a cellmate and goes out for Rec for one hour a day at different times. There are six men in each cage. It just so happens they put one bad person in there with you. There are 6-7 cages. Living by the code and politics of good standing white guys get a bad person put in their cage, and if you don't hit them, it puts you in violation of the code. If you ever land in another cage, the other white guys would be obligated to hit you. We woke up at six am when the lights came on. They would have a Rec Officer on the Unit doing Rec sign-up. If your cell did not meet the requirements to have Rec Privilege, you would lose your privilege to go to Rec that day. For example, if you had something hanging on the walls or your bed was not made, and your cell was dirty in any way. You'd be locked in your cell for twenty-three hours without Rec. In the cell, there were no hooks to hang clothes after a shower. You're only allowed to use the shower three times a week, Monday, Wednesday, and Friday. The other Unit was allowed to use the shower Tuesday, Thursday, and Saturday. No one was allowed o use the shower on Sunday. Every two weeks, you would rotate one cell from the left to the right. After your cell rotates, you and your cell-mate get all your stuff together. Then you would clean the cell toilet and sink and floor etc.; We were lucky if you had good neighbors on either side that you rotate behind because there are some people that have no consideration for the next man who would be moving into your cell.

The SMU is in disciplinary lockdown. There are a lot of different incidents that take place or what any one person does to get designated to the Special Management Unit. Shots are a name for disciplinary action. One hundred series are the most severe, like 104 series is a knife in possession, and 101 is using a knife to injure, stab, or kill someone. Drug shots, I believe, are 107. Fighting is 201 or 224. Some inmates get designated for making alcohol, dirty urine, drug introduction, or simply just having a lot of influence to be able to state group demonstrations. They have 205 series shots for inmates that masturbate and play with themselves in front of the female staff. There are all kinds of stuff.

We wake up in the morning and make a cup of coffee from serving us breakfast. We would save the cardboard milk carton. With the aluminum fish pack from the commissary, you would wash the pack, turn it inside out, fill it with water, light the carton on fire, and that would heat the water for your cup of coffee. Sometimes you would get pulled before they served you breakfast, so mostly after breakfast.

On your unit of tier, you have all the good-standing white guys who talk with each other. They all meet up, talk or work out together during the Rec hour when it's too cold outside on the tier by, screaming out the door in the vent. Because there's a lot of communication in the vent, you can talk to your neighbor next door and the two cells above you. There are phases you need to complete to get to the SMU Phase. There are programs you have to complete to get to the phase of each different course. In cases where you don't understand the program, you'll be set back ninety days.

Shane is not allowed to send an email home, and he can only call me on the sixteenth and at the end of the month. The money I put in his commissary pays for the calls, which are about three dollars per call. The phone calls are supposed to be fifteen minutes long, but they always seem to hang up at ten. The Commissary is very expensive, and the parents are responsible for it. You can only buy certain things at the store. This has cost me thousands of dollars a year with that and the calls and emails. My son's property has been lost on two occasions. This happened when he was moved from one prison to another or was sent to segregation, and his property was packed up. I am not the only parent this has happened to. Parents end up having to replace everything. With all the money the taxpayers send to these prisons, it should not cost us, families. They should be able to talk to the families for free and as much as they can during their free time. During the time my son was in the SMU, he would hear the screaming of inmates that were shackled; they would take the men and put them on a stretcher and put the cuffs so tight their hands and wrists would swell, and the guards would punch them in the stomach then tightened the chain around their stomach even worse, leave them like that for days. The reason they did this was that they would masturbate in front of the women, and if the inmate covered their windows up, guards would dress up in their gear and charge in and restrain them. No addict or non-violent drug offender should have to endure this. Most COs should be behind bars for abuse, misconduct, and bringing it in themselves.

Shane is doing some type of psychology packets like workbooks and has to go through phases to finish the program at SMU. It can take nine to twenty-four months. Shane is starting his fifth month.

While he was there, I received a letter from the warden, and with the letter was a copy of the email I sent to President Trump. Letter from the warden.

This is what I received from the warden:

U.S. Department of Justice
Federal Bureau of Prisons
Administrative United States
Penitentiary
1100 Cine Mile Road
PO Box 1001
Office of Warden
Thomson, IL 61265
December 12, 2019

Ms. Denise Hansen
89 Rantoul St. Apt. 315
Beverly, MA. 01915
Subject: WH20015550

Dear Ms. Denise Hansen,

This letter is to provide a response to an inquiry regarding inmate Hansen, Shane, Register No. 95415-038, ability to participate in Drug Programming. Records indicate Mr. Hansen was interviewed by the Drug Abuse Program Coordinator (DAPC), at the Federal Correction Complex (FCC), Hazelton, West Virginia, on October 15, 2019, and found qualified to participate in the Residential Drug Abuse Program (RDAP). Currently, Mr. Hansen has been placed in the Special Management Program (SMU) at the Administrative United States Penitentiary (AUSP), Thomson, Illinois. While in this program, Mr. Hansen is not able to participate in the ADAP PROGRAM. However, after successful completion of the SMU program, should there be enough time remaining in his sentence, Mr. Hansen can be transferred to a facility to participate in the program. I am pleased to see that Mr. Hansen successfully completed Non-Residential Drug Abuse Treatment on November 8, 2017. It is highly recommended Mr. Hansen continues to take his recovery seriously and work with Psychology services while in the SMU program to address any substance abuse issues.

I trust that this will address any concerns you have regarding Mr. Hansen's access to substance treatment.

Sincerely,

C. Rivers, Warden

The email that I had written to President Trump was with the letter written above to me from his warden. I was shocked that the President did this for me. MY EMAIL BELOW WAS IN WITH THE LETTER I HAD WRITTEN TO PRESIDENT TRUMP.

From: The White House (mail agent) (no reply@contact.whitehouse .gov.)
Sent: Tuesday, November 12, 2019, 11:54 PM
To: DOJExec.Sec (JMD)
Subject: Case #20015550- New Case Assignment (Intranet Quorum IMA00112143)

THE WHITE HOUSE
WASHINGTON

Case ID: 2001550
From: Ms. Denise Hansen
Submitted: 11/22/19 11:23 PM
Email: denisehansen25@yahoo.com
Phone: 978-394-1665
Address: 89 Rantoul Street, Apt. 315, Beverly, MA 01915-4239
Message: Dear President Trump,

I have written you letters and sent you emails. I need help for my son. He never hurt anyone except himself. The last crime that put him in the federal prison system was a one-time possession of a firearm. It was his friend's gun who was with him. It was another friend that set him up to sell the gun to the other.

He had a few drug charges in the past but never large amounts. He's been using heroin since he was eighteen. He is an addict, a sick man that needs help.

He is being transferred to an SMU (Special Management Unit), where he's waiting in Oklahoma City FTC transfer. He's waiting to go to SMU because he relapsed two times in six years. He was sentenced to ten years. This never should have gone to a federal level in the first place. He needs treatment. Treatment does not mean having to be locked up in a cage twenty-three hours a day. He's been in one since June 23rd. He's been in jail since July 18, 2013.

Now, the SMU will keep him locked up twenty-three hours a day. He's already been locked up for nine months. That's a total of fourteen months of confinement. This is not good for an addict. He needs productivity and treatment. They will not give it to him. He's a good kid with a big heart but has a sickness that needs to be addressed. These USP Penitentiaries are no place for them. In God's name, please fix this long segregation of addicts, and please get him the help he needs.

I love you and your beautiful wife, who are keeping these damn drugs out and helping mothers not have babies that are addicted.

We need a new pill and need to get rid of the ones with opiates in them. Please help my son. He's spent six years and four months in prison, locked down 24/7. He couldn't even finish getting a GED because he was locked down so much. Please help him so he's not locked up like an animal. His name is Shane Hansen (95415038).

I'm reaching out to you as a mother who has been advocating for addiction for sixteen years. Stop the legalization of needles!

Thank you

It was so upsetting to me after I read the letter from the warden. There is no help for his addiction. This is where the system fails him again.

Shane's out date is July 22, 2022, but hopefully, he'll be assigned to the halfway house for the 149 days of the good time he has left. My son writes to me every chance he can and calls me twice a month. He says he's okay so far, but his being locked up twenty-three hours every day keeps me awake at night. I worry about everything, and I don't understand why addicts are not placed where they can get the help they need. My son never hurt anyone, and he was sentenced to ten years. So many people have done worse, and the Trump Prison Reform Bill is supposed to help non-violent drug offenders. I write to President Trump every week, asking him to help. He wrote me a letter and, in the letter, he quotes, "To treat all drug users." So, why are they not listening? They did nothing that Trump Wanted.

This is a copy of the letter I received from President Trump:

WASHINGTON
August 6, 2019

Ms. Denise Hansen
Beverly, Massachusetts

Dear Ms. Hansen,
Thank you for taking the time to express your views regarding criminal justice and prison reform.
For too long, the Federal criminal justice system has imposed overly punitive sentences on nonviolent drug offenders. One significant way to make our justice system fairer is by reforming mandatory minimum sentences, which have had a disproportionate impact on certain communities and increased prison overcrowding and costs. For this reason, I was pleased to sign into law the bipartisan FIRST STEP Act, which reduces the enhanced penalties for certain repeat drug offenders and eliminates the three-strike mandatory life sentence provision. The legislation also broadens the existing safety valve that allows judges to impose a sentence that is below the mandatory minimum for nonviolent drug offenders with little to no criminal history. Further, it allows certain drug offenders to petition courts for a review of their

entence, including public safety, criminal history, and the nature of he offense.

More than a third of former Federal prisoners are rearrested within five years after their release. As a Nation, we must help break this vicious cycle. Offering those who have been held accountable for their crimes an opportunity to be contributing members of society is a critical element of criminal justice that can reduce our crime rates and prison populations, decrease burdens to the American taxpayer, and make our country safer.

The FIRST STEP Act makes reforms that will help prepare inmates to become contributing members of society and avoid subsequent incarceration. This legislation expands prison employment program opportunities, offers improved opportunities for inmates to engage in education coursework and vocational training, and establishes pilot programs to earn time credits to apply towards prerelease custody or supervised release. Additionally, it requires the Bureau of Prisons to develop a plan to improve access to medication-assisted treatment for Heroin and other opioid abuse.

Thank you for writing. To learn more about what my Administration is doing to help prisoners reenter society as productive, law-abiding, please visit www.WhiteHouse.gov. As President, I am committed to making our Federal Justice system fairer and our communities safer. Sincerely,

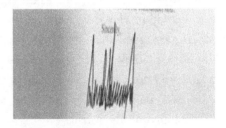

This was a letter I received from President Trump. I voted for this president, and I am happy with everything he's done. I will be voting for him in the next election, but more needs to be done to make the

justice system fair. The justice system is not giving addicts the productivity they need and counseling every day. Why can they not make parts for a business or learn a trade to make them a better person? They cannot be a better person in society without a job or a place to live. The reason for this is they don't get any help. They are locked up like animals and are set up, so they fail.

In January 2020, we started dealing with a virus that came over from China. It's called Coronavirus or COVID-19. We have not seen anything of this magnitude since the Influenza in 1918. President Trump has been utilizing all of his resources. He closed the borders within a few days of the first reported case. The President has a task force that works with him every day. He just recently enacted the Defense Production Act.

The virus has been crippling our economy forcing businesses to close, and a lot of employees are being laid off or just losing their jobs. Congress put together a 2.2 trillion-dollar Stimulus Package to help workers and businesses. This will give direct payments to families. On March 27, 2020, President Trump approved and signed the bill.

My biggest concern is that AG William Barr spoke about releasing inmates that are sixty and over, non-violent with underlying conditions. Why isn't he talking about releasing all the non-violent prisoners? My son is in a situation where he is confined twenty-four hours a day because of the virus. As of now, ten federal prisons have the virus in there. My son will be thirty-five in June. Viruses hit every age, not just the elderly. My son had covid in The SMU, but luckily was not serious.

When President Trump signed the First Step Act (Prison Reform Bill), I thought I understood they were going to release non-violent drug offenders. My son was not charged in federal court for a violent crime. Why does the BOP call possession of a firearm violent that never hurt anyone or shot anyone so violent?

I am praying for my son's safety and to come home to be the best man he can be for himself and for his son Cody which he has not spoken to since 2014. The probate family courts are not fair to the other parent. Talking and seeing your son helps the incarcerated one and helps the child understand and still love his absent parent. The loss of his son devastated Shane. I also lost my grandson because of his and his mom's reasons. I am still trying to figure it out. I could never understand why. I always had my grandson with me on Christmas. I miss my grandson coming over to open up his gifts. I miss not having my family over for Christmas dinner. For the last five years, I've not put up a Christmas tree. Yes, my life sucks! Yes, my son made some bad choices. For the last seven years, I've been serving time with my son. I haven't been able to focus on anything for myself or relationships. I am not making excuses for him, but everyone needs to understand addiction is a disease and should be treated like one.

Shane gets allowed only two phone calls a month. I think the inmates should be able to call more often and talk longer. Now, I worry more about him with this Coronavirus. Just recently, back on February 5, 2020, six inmates became disruptive in a cage where they get their rec time for an hour a day. My son lost twenty-seven days of good time. He also lost the phone and his commissary through June 23rd. I just received a letter from my son. He apologized, and he said, "I was in a cage with no way out at all. It was three on three. All I could do was fight to protect myself, which I did. I'm not going to be the one that gets my head stomped onto the ground until my eyes pop out of my head. Sorry, I want to make it home with all my body parts. I know I have to be good and get home to you and my son Cody. This shit happens in these places. I've been doing everything well. I've gotten a hundred on my last five assignments, extra Psychology work, and doing all programs and more. Mom. I'm sorry I love you."

My son also told me in his letter that when he went in front of the DHO (disciplinary), he begged the woman not to take his phone away because my mother is over sixty and he was worried about me, and the woman didn't care and took his phone privileges away. This frustrates me because he lost commissary, good time, and phone over something he had no control over. They should not make a family member or an inmate suffer during a pandemic. I guess I have to live with their decision, being stressed out and not being able to talk to my son during these hard times. In my heart, I believe they do this on purpose, so they lose their good time and can't come home early. I feel with the prisons; it's all about money.

I spoke to his Counselor, Mr. Hammond, one of the best counselors I ever talked to, and he assured me Shane was doing well and doing everything they could to prevent the virus from coming in there.

I pray to God for his safety every night.

My son was not charged in the federal court for a violent crime. So why does the BOP (Bureau of Prisons) consider his charges a violent crime? He never hurt anybody or attempted to hurt anybody.

I, as his mom, did everything to fight for him. I fixed the federal court mistakes. I got charges dismissed from the Annie Dookhan case. I advocated so many times for drug awareness and spoke at the vigil. I did all this because I love my son. Being alone all my nights, all I do is think about my boy, and tears come running down my cheeks from worry. Hopefully, I will be here for him when he comes home. Shane sent me many loving, caring cards to express how thankful he was to have me.

My son transferred to USP Beaumont, Texas.

January 20, 2021, my son was transferred to Beaumont, Texas. I thought to myself, '*OMG! He's going to another terrible place*'. Shane was put into an RDAP program. He would never have been able to finish the program with the time he had left with all the damn lock-downs. My son transferred to an open cell in CB block, where he finished his time.

Less than a month later, a very bad snowstorm hit. Talk about bad luck. The inmates were given three bottled glasses of water a day, and there was no commissary. They were locked in their cells for quite some time. At first, it was two months, and then for the next six months, it was modified to two hours a day. They had to boil water to wash. The conditions were horrible. The toilets wouldn't flush. There were no phone calls; it took weeks to receive any letters. There were cockroaches big enough to carry a cinnamon bun. I worried and night for their safety. For a mother, the worrying never end..

COVID kept the inmates in lockdown as much as possible while the guards walked around with no masks. Our loved ones suffered as a result of this. Lockdowns are not the answer. My son contracted COVID at SMU and again in Texas. There were vaccinations available, but my son doesn't believe in them.

The stabbings and killing of inmates went on. An inmate was stabbed on July 21, 2021, and was left in critical condition. Less than a month later, on August 16th, there were two more stabbings. One inmate died, and he had little time left to serve. He was thirty-three years old. I was very upset with the stabbings, lockdowns, and what they fed the inmates. My son called me and said, "Mom, I want to come home. It's terrible here. I never want to come back."

My son signed his paperwork for the HWH (Halfway house) on September 16th. He was told it might take 'till October to get his release date.

There was another lockdown on October 1, 2021. Some inmates had Covid. A few of the inmates were brought to the hospital. The inmates started coming out of their cells twenty minutes at a time. There were no phone calls or emails allowed. It took days to get emails or calls. There were long segregations.

Starting October 8th, I started calling Texas Senator Webber's office three or four times a week, and I complained of the horrific conditions. The inmates were fed bologna and peanut butter sandwiches every day. The Senator's office kept telling me they were short of staff, and that's why they weren't getting back to me. The guards were the ones bringing in the COVID.

USP Beaumont was the worst of the five prisons Shane has been in. During the last year, he was only out four times a full day for rec and sun. COVID spreads more with lockdowns than with being outside. The guards were lazy and let everything slide. My son finally got his out date for March 14, 2022, and his release date for August 14th.

On January 31, 2022, two inmates were murdered, and the prison went into another lockdown. This time it lasted for months. I became friends with so many moms, Ashley, Ethel, Sabrina, Tina, and another woman named Jeanette from West Virginia. We met on a Facebook website. I don't know how any of us could get through the pain if it wasn't for talking to these lovely people. We talked to one another to see if any of us had heard from their loved ones. If you called the prison, the phone didn't get answered. If the phone did get answered, you would ask for their counselor, and you heard click, click, click for ten minutes. Then the call went to voicemail, but there was no return phone call.

The letters we received were either an empty envelope or a taped one. Most of the time, we didn't receive anything for weeks. The inmates were losing weight from the lack of food they were being fed. They had money in their commissary but were not allowed to go. If they were, there was a fifty-dollar limit in which we all knew the cost of food went up.

I called Senator Lee's office. I sent emails to Senator Durbin's office, and I wrote to the judiciary committee. I talked to Senator Webber's office more than a dozen times. So, what's keeping them in a 6'x9' cell day after day, night after night? NOBODY CARED! Senator Durbin had a judiciary committee meeting. He said, "Sixty thousand inmates have not received their program credits." They still haven't, and my son never received his.

In 2018 President Trump signed into law to give the inmates their credit and treat them as inmates with addiction. No, they punished them instead. An inmate was not supposed to be located any more than five hundred miles from home. My son never was.

There's a prisoner in there that's eighty-four years old. He is serving thirty-three years for drugs which is a non-violent crime. I think he should be allowed to come home.

My son sent that box of his pictures and meaningful things out of prison before the lockdown on January 31st. I complained about that every day, and they kept saying, "Oh, we sent it out." Three weeks

ater, I called again, and I was told, "It's in my office." I r⌐
⌐ox a week after my son was home.

My son was supposed to come home on March 14th. I was ⌐⌐
⌐or him to get on the bus. I was up all night. There was no call the next
morning. I was upset, worried, and crying. I called the damn place, and
there was no answer. I called again, and a man answered. I asked to
⌐peak to Ms. Harley, his case worker. The man that answered was the
⌐ne that was supposed to send Shane's box back before the lockdown. I
⌐eceived the box four months later.

Shane was supposed to leave the prison on March 14th. He didn't
⌐et to leave when he was supposed to because his paperwork was
messed up. I was up all night worrying. I had no call from them telling
me Shane was on his way. I was so upset. They screwed up his paperwork, and they had months to figure it out. A week later, on March
21st, Shane was put on a Greyhound bus to come home. That was a
twenty-nine-hour ride to Boston, MA. I felt that was ridiculous. They
⌐ould have at least flown him home halfway. Shane was using other
⌐eople's phones, and I was getting calls from him telling me where he
⌐vas and that he was safe.

The next morning, March 22[nd,] around 9:30, I received a call from
Shane. He told me the bus was hijacked in Gwinnett County in Atlanta,
Georgia, on I-85. The driver of the bus ran off the bus and left the bus
⌐oor locked with the gunman inside. The bus was going from Atlanta,
GA, to New York. There were kids and other people on the bus. My
⌐on was brave and told the gunman, "You don't want to do this. I just
⌐erved ten years for a gun charge. I just want to go home." He also told
⌐he gunman, who seemed young, "I need to get my insulin from under
⌐he bus, or I will die. (Shane was not on insulin) I haven't taken it for
⌐wo hours." Shane asked, "Can I exit out the hatch door?"

The gunman first said, "No," and then he said, "Yes." My son took a
⌐hance and opened the hatch. He then jumped off the top of the bus. The
⌐unman didn't shoot anyone. Some people followed Shane out of the
⌐atch, and some climbed out the windows. My son and others could

have been killed. Shane was the first one out of the bus. He jumped off the bus and saw the SWAT team coming down the road. He was hoping that they didn't think it was him and that he was the one doing the hijacking. Everyone thanked my son for talking to the gunman. The bus was laid up there for three hours. The gunman had to be gassed out. They fed the passengers as they waited for the bus to be cleared out. The bus driver should have been charged for leaving the inside, but none of the people I talked to could press legal charges against the driver. This was the help of God. That gunman could have killed innocent people.

Shane and the others waited for another bus. A bus finally
up. Shane borrowed a cell phone from someone and let me know he
was okay. He called me again at nine at night from a bus station in
Charlotte, North Carolina. He was getting a new itinerary. My son had
to stay there all night until eleven the next morning. The bus was to go
to Virginia from there. There would have been a three-hour layover in
New York until 2:00 am. I was worried sick with all the crime there
and the ordeal he just went through. Shane asked me to pick him up in
Washington, DC, around eight PM. He had to sleep on a bench that
night in Charlotte, NC. There were people smoking crack. Needless to
say, he didn't get much that night. People were coming in and out
while he slept on a bench, and some people were doing drugs. Not a
good sight for him to see

I didn't want to make the drive alone, so I called an old friend of
mine named Joe to take a ride with me to Washington, DC. I picked
Joe up in Salem, MA., at 6:30, and then we drove straight through. We
stopped an hour away, had something to eat, and then went to the bus
station. Ashley, an inmate's mom, kept track of Shane's schedule to let
me know when the bus would pull up. We sat in my car in front of the
station for an hour. We were fortunate that we were not asked to move.

I had to tell Shane's probation officer and lawyer that I was picking
him up. I didn't want this to happen again because of the rising crimes
in New York.

Shane is still under the BOP (Bureau of Prisons) until August 14,
2022. Shane was supposed to be at the Halfway House the next day. He
never would have arrived on time if I hadn't picked him up.

Ashley was one of the people I met on My Group on Facebook.
Her husband still remains in Beaumont. She kept track of my son's
itinerary and the bus number and kept track of it on her computer. She
was a big help.

Joe and I waited outside the bus terminal. The bus was supposed to
come in at 8:20 pm. Ashley called me, and it said it was coming at
7:50. I was so afraid someone was going to kick us out of the great
parking spot we found. I ran inside and made sure I was at the right

place. Then, the people I saw were begging for money. I was very nervous after what happened in Atlanta. My friend Joe waited for me in the car. I told him I'd be right back. It was a huge bus station with escalators, food places, and people coming and going. I was so nervous.

I asked someone where the buses came in. A man told me to follow him. Then he pointed upstairs. When I reached the top of the stairs, there were people all standing around waiting, and there were different parking terminals for the different buses that would be arriving. A man that worked there directed me to where the bus would come in from Charlotte, NC. He said, "It should arrive over there in five minutes," as he pointed to the terminal.

I waited patiently. I was so nervous but at the same time the happiest I'd been in ten years. My heart was throbbing. The bus pulled up right in that five-minute time. I was waiting as people came off the bus. I was thinking and praying it was the right one. Shane finally walked down the stairs of the Greyhound bus. My son was home and safe. He walked down the stairs wearing a pair of gray sweatpants and a white tee-shirt, and sneakers, carrying a bag. We gave each other a big hug. We talked about the crazy hijacking as we walked the stairs to meet Joe, who was waiting outside at the curb. I was so glad that it was worth the long ride because of what happened to him in Atlanta, Georgia. I could not stop looking at him, for I hadn't seen him in two years.

We started walking out to the car and through the bus terminal when Shane stopped and gave an old man, a homeless person, a pair of sweatpants and a sweatshirt. He has a big heart. The man was so appreciative.

Joe and I drove twenty-five hours up and back. We made a few stops along the way, and I did all the driving. He changed the clothes he's been in for a couple of days after one stop. That is when we took a picture of us together. The ride home in the pouring rain was hell. We were all exhausted. It was ten long years of hell, and I was right there with him. Shane sat in front of me and Joe in the back; I could not see a thing. It was raining so hard, and tractor-trailer trucks were blasting us by and blowing their horn to move out of the slow lane and trying to listen to the GPS at the same time. I just wanted to get us home safe. Shane never stopped talking and ate everything he could on the way home, the food he had never got to eat for ten years. He was so happy to eat, and having a real cup of coffee was great for my son while I drove to get us home safely.

After that long ride, we dropped my son off at the Halfway house at 5:30 that next morning. I bought a lot of clothes for my son to start out with. I had some old things that I had kept in storage for ten years, knowing lots were not in style anymore. Some things I brought to him were not allowed, like a certain material, a blanket, and I do not understand that. Kept an iPhone 11 for him, which I turned on and put in my name until he got on his feet. It was really tough for me to try to help him and his son. I paid his fines and renewed his license. Shane can now renew his license himself in June of 2022.

During his stay at the halfway house, I called the Coolidge House in Boston, MA, on Huntington Ave; he had a few odd experiences. My son first had some guy come up to him and ask him if he wanted any drugs. My son said he showed him a picture of something that may crush pills on his cell phone. Shane said no, I do no not know what that is, he guessed it was an undercover cop trying to get him in trouble, but my son was too smart to fall into it or want a damn thing to do with it. The Halfway house in Boston was not the best place; they really tried to find things to put them back where they came from.

I bought my son some Whey protein so he could lock it up in the YMCA, which was located across the street where he worked out. They didn't allow food in the place, so my son would take a little back to the house so he could mix it with his milk and have it for breakfast. All they had was muffins and stuff, so my son would drink protein instead. Shane used a plastic spoon to scoop it out of the baggie he had brought back from the gym. He came back to the house and found they had taken all his blankets from his bed and the spoon because the powder dried up, so they thought it was drugs. How wrong they were, you cannot cook drugs on a plastic spoon, and they ended up giving him his blankets back at a later time. They took his vitamins that I spent twenty bucks on and never returned them. I gave them to him because it was good to take vitamins because of Covid. He was never violated, but it seems to me they tried hard enough to do so. He did all the right things.

Shane started looking for a job and went to an interview at a lumber yard where my son knew everything. He was experienced in all that construction stuff. My ex-husband Ray taught him a lot since he was fifteen years old. They would not hire him because of his criminal ecord. After spending ten years of your life, this should all be off your record (Cory) so he and all inmates coming home can get on their feet. Why should they still have to pay for his crimes when he already had o for ten years?

Shane's co-defendant from Florida is doing excellent. He found omeone to help my son. Shane started landscaping, making good pay. Shane worked hard, never missed a day of work, and took the train very day. He lasted three months. Taylor, the same person, moved him o a contracting job where he is today. Shane is on three years' probation. Hopefully, they'll let him off sooner.

I helped Shane get a down payment for his truck. I co-signed for im; now he has transportation. And Shane left the HWH on Aug 12, 2022. He lives with his girlfriend, Jen. They had been girlfriend and boyfriend when they were fourteen and met up again on Facebook. The probation cleared the home with approval. Jen is a great girl. I give all my support to him and will continue to do so until I can no longer. Shane sees his boy Cody and is good friends with his son's mom. My son has a great job and moved up to a contracting company, thanks to his good friends Shawn and Taylor. It is now January 2023, and I couldn't be prouder of him as I am today. Shane and his son Cody are closer today; they made up for lost time.

My feelings about What I Went Through and the Changes That Need to Be Made In the BOP.

Other mothers, myself, fathers, and grandparents, what we experienced from the BOP is inhumane treatment. It was deplorable what we heard from our loved ones and what we read from articles from the BOP and USP news. It is unacceptable what we read on My Group on Facebook and the sad stories of the moms talking about the treatment their loved ones are getting.

First, I want to say the BOP does not have treatment for addiction. They will tell you there is, but they'll lie and say that there is no time for treatment. The lockdowns last for months at a time. The inmates do not have time to finish anything. They cannot go to a class to learn a trade or earn a GED in a USP penitentiary.

The murders and the stabbings keep the inmates locked down for months at a time. So how could anyone think the lifers would not act up after being in a cell day after day, night after night? Then they modify the inmates coming out like two hours a unit at a time.

There's no sunlight, fresh air, or hot meals. The inmates are given peanut butter that will not spread enough on a piece of bread. They're given bologna sandwiches and cheese that taste like rubber. Powdered milk for their cereal which they would poop white. The packets measure 2 "both length and width, and they are filled halfway.

The inmates eat this stuff and lose weight because they are fed this every day. Some prisons will make them skip meals and will not feed them a meal. Where is all the money going? When or if there is not a lockdown, their daily schedule will go like this in most all USP high max prisons, at 5:45 am, they open cell doors, breakfast is at 6:00 am, and then lunch is at 10:30 am. Supper is available at 4:00 pm. That is quite a long time between lunch and supper. Luckily most of them get commissary, and the ones that have no families would not get anything. They would get showers three times a week. Monday, Wednesday, and Friday. When they were in lockdowns, they were lucky to get a shower unless they were out an hour a day or two hours. They got their showers, then. Forget the fresh air. They're all about money, taking their commissary away after we, the families, pay for them, true-links the phone calls they charge the families, including the computer and email. They rip the families off when they punish the inmates. The system is corrupt. Drug addicts with gun possessions never hurt anyone, but they get put in the same prisons as murderers and rapists, MS-13s, and other gang members that most are doing life. Most addicts are non-violent offenders. Like that man in his late eighties, why can he not go home to spend his last dying days with his children? Thirty-three years for selling drugs but then again, they are allowed drugs pouring over our borders. People like him who are non-violent should be allowed to go home. Why should they die in prison for a non-violent crime? Thirty-three years is a long time; I would assume he's rehabilitated himself by now.

The guards at Texas BOP Beaumont do not wear masks. They're lazy and let things slide. They just had an overdose in June 2022, where the inmate died. There are many drugs inside but no visits because of lockdowns. What does that tell me? It tells me the dirty guards bring them in. When an inmate dies, a family member is the emergency contact. Well, if you hear about murder and you call Texas Beaumont. Good luck getting in touch with someone. They never answer the phones there. I and others could not get a hold of their case managers. A friend of mine's son was stabbed thirteen times. Another inmate's mom called her to give her the bad news. She had to drive all the way to Texas to find out if he was alright. My son, in his ten years, had not been able to get his teeth cleaned. The COs lie to you when you call. Families are important to both them and the inmate. Telephone calls are taken away. Visits are also taken away because of lockdowns. This is not humane, and the families and their children suffer.

Addicts and low-point offenders SHOULD NOT be put in a USP Penitentiary.

They treat families like we're to blame. The families are locked up with their loved ones every day. Cost us, families, 1000's a year for their little or no food commissary. If they're out of lockdown, you worry about them being hurt or, even worse, dead. President Trump signed into law to give addicts the help they need, as you read in this letter.

The inmates are supposed to be within five hundred miles of their homes. That never happened with my son. The last year for Shane, he was in Beaumont, eighteen hundred miles away. Prior to that, the other four prisons were more than five hundred miles from home which were insane. Families need contact with their loved ones and vice versa.

All USP Prisons are locked down during every damn holiday. They cannot talk to their kids or any loved ones at home, especially at Christmas. Not one holiday are they allowed a phone call.

The letters take weeks for you to receive them. Sometimes you get them, and they're just an empty envelope. There are times when fifteen days go by without any mail. The First and Eighth amendment reads no cruelty and abuse.

The majority of the states do not allow solitary confinement for more than fifteen days. The inmates stay in a small cell for up to twenty-three hours a day. Sometimes for months. Their symptoms for just fifteen days can cause psychological damage ranging from anxiety to paranoia to inability to have coherent thoughts. It's much worse for the ones that are already mentally ill. Most of addicts in prolonged solitary confinement can cause a relapse. This is why segregation among the inmates needs to STOP! Some I know have PTSD.

The guards turned the air conditioning up and made the inmates stay in their shorts and tee shirts while the guards walked around with hats and coats. The inmates lit fires under their asses to keep warm. Drones are bringing drugs in, and guards sell phones to inmates for like $900 bucks, and what if the guards on the towers do not see the drones? I believe they know everything and lock them down for their own corrupt doing. Then they have shakedowns and punish inmates for things that some dirty guards are responsible for.

I spoke to one of the wives the week before her husband was released. She told me her husband refused to go back to his dorm. He wanted to avoid any problems because he was in fear for his life, and the CO looked at him and said, "'I don't give a fuck about you!" Then the CO slammed him on his face and shackled him. Next, he was brought to protective custody. He wanted to go home. A parent called me today, and the USP Beaumont Texas inmates had no hot water for three weeks; how inhumane. Sixty thousand or more inmates never received their good time for programs they could finish. My son did 300 hours total and never got time off for them. Why is it that if your points are at twenty-three, which puts an inmate in a medium facility, why are they not moving them to that facility? They keep them in a dangerous high max which is wrong! Sixteen points are low, and twenty-three is medium. Anything over is high max.

Being in prison for what I saw and heard, read by other moms' comments, and what I had been through with my son is a very sick and ugly way of rehabilitating someone. Did any of them in the USP ever get a GED or a program finished? The answer is no. They come home with no place to go most of them and very difficult to find a job with benefits. The rents are ridiculously high, and with no training in prison, how are they supposed to make it outside? That's why many prisoners return back into the prison system because the system fails them. I am still very concerned about all the inmates in these prisons, their health, the treatment they do not receive, for example, teeth cleaning, proper nutrition, and inhumane treatment on every level, and their insanity, most of all, for months of long segregation. The district attorneys, the judges that give these long sentences, a person or persons with a drug problem who does not get the help they need, whether it is suboxone or programming, what is wrong with this system? Men and women are in high max prison for selling drugs and getting years, yet they allow open borders with Fentanyl, Heroin, and Meth that are killing our young children. Maybe they need to close the borders and allow these men and women that are serving twenty to thirty years to be able to GO HOME, for I say it's our laws to be blamed for. Maybe if our borders had been closed years ago, this problem with our addicted kids might not have happened. Legalizing syringes was wrong. That leaves needles all over our streets, and the needles get shared. Now there are more overdoses that occur. They used to charge you a year in prison. Close the borders and allow these men and women that are serving twenty to thirty years to be able to go home non-violent. I say it's something our laws are to be blamed for. Maybe we should go back to these laws.

I live in Massachusetts, and if you were to drive by Mass Avenue in Boston like my son does every day on his way to work, he would show me a video of all the addicts lined up on the street selling drugs, sticking needles in each other like their neck or wherever their vein had not already collapsed. It's just like Chicago and San Francisco; nobody cares. These are useless Democrat cities with the worst people running them. They allow this instead of putting them in a county jail for sixty days and cleaning them up. Let them go through their withdrawals, help them by giving them some meds to ease the pain, and then to a treatment program. Most county jails are supposed to have sections for addicts and offer them some kind of blocker when they leave. This will help most addicts and give them the chance to stay clean. Most addicts hate their lives chasing drugs and owing money. Most lose lots of friends from overdoses. As I mentioned earlier, in most Democratic states, their representatives do not care and do nothing about it. This is one mom that gives a damn and fights for years.

I spoke to other inmates that I wrote to, and I grew to care about them. They loved my son and thought his mom was a great mama dook, as they would say, and they are telling me that the commissary is going up forty-five cents for one soup and seventy cents for a cup of soup and you can get a whole case at the dollar store is what they tell me and the size of it all is ridiculous. This system is so corrupt in many ways, like sentencing others differently for the same crime because they might be of a different color or have no money to pay their awyers. Drug sentences are way too long when President Biden's dministration is allowing millions of fentanyl over our border, and oung as thirteen-year-olds are dying and some infants. The injection ites, and the legalization of syringes, made our drug problem worse. Addicts will always share needles. Mass Ave in Boston, MA, is a sight or sore eyes, seeing tents and people laying around, sitting around vith needles in their arms and some nodded out, and the cops sitting here watching until someone overdoses; what a sad country, yes my on video it as he drove by there while staying at the HWH which is a iome they go to under the BOP. Homeless people are everywhere, yet nany illegals are pouring in with their drug cartels and getting beau- iful hotels to stay in, but no one cares about our children's homeless American children. I have a family member who desperately needs a alace to live. This makes me very upset. Building homes for the home- ess and helping the addicts into treatment, and having no injection ites. Injection sites are putting poison in our children's bodies, and teeping them addicted is horrible. This is not our America. Rent :ontrol is what we need. Very sad days ahead. If President Biden can oay billions to let student loans be forgiven, then why can he not build reatment facilities to get these addicts off the streets that today, the ear 2022, is made worse by open borders? Fentanyl is killing more oday than any year. The administration today don't care about the lives ost from drugs. I am not trying to be political, but the truth is President Trump did care, and I loved his policies.

My hope, prayers, and best wishes are with my son Shane and anyone battling addiction. Anyone with this disease, please seek help. Parents, please support your child. Do not give up. Fight like you never fought before. Addiction is a disease. People in government need to start treating it like one. As I mentioned in my book, prison is not the answer; treatment is. The families left behind by a child that overdoses are the ones that will suffer for the rest of their lives. I have been to many funerals, and it just breaks your heart. My son told me he is glad he served ten years. He believes it saved his life not only from Heroin but the deadly Fentanyl that is out there today and is killing so many young kids. It is October 2022. They don't even talk about it on the fake news. I made calls to Mayor Wu's office in Boston and the DA office to clean up Mass Ave. Put these addicts in treatment for as long as it takes to clean them up so they can get on Suboxone to help them stay alive and give them a chance. Leaving them out on the streets sets a bad example.

For all the families and friends who have loved ones that you care about, please watch over them. If any of you even think your loved ones have changed in their behavior, check their eyes; large pupils cocaine, tiny pupils especially means opioids, when they stay small even in the dark. Check their rooms, under the flap of their sneakers, for where they hid the drugs. The bottom of an empty Arizona iced tea can be used to cook dope spoons in their room. Check suspended ceilings where needles can be hidden. Look above the doors. Parents have to be aware and talk to their children about the dangers of drugs.

Whatever color an individual is, it should not matter how much time they do, but it should be equal to anyone else's time for the same crime. I was fighting for my son's treatment, as you have read, to get him the treatment he deserved because of his sickness, but if you have money, it seems to me that they get off easy than anyone that does not have money. Why is this justice? Let me give you an example that was already on the news. Taylor Wesley of Ohio killed his mom, stabbed her to death, and he only was given nineteen years, nine more than my son and many more for nonviolent offenses. There are many more like him. The justice system is not fair and needs fixing. Some on death row are most probably innocent, and they need to go back to some of these cases and check the DNA. "Trial by Fire" was a movie about an innocent man from Texas who they turned a blind eye to and put an innocent man to death. The governor knew he was innocent and left him to die anyway. This was a true story.

I just heard on the news that Hunter deserves treatment instead of ten years. This upset me. Shane served ten years. Hunter's crime is worth ten years. I fought years calling Congress and the State Reps trying to get the same for my son, so I'll be damned if Hunter gets away with his crime.

Today's President, our 46th, to make it clear, wants to pardon all pot dealers. That's a good thing since it's legal in most states, and inmates must spend over ten years or more for their crimes. My question is this: Why is he such a hypocrite when all the dope dealers who are non-violent who had spent twenty or thirty years in prison? Some of them are in their late 80s. Since this 46th President allows the damn drugs to come over our border? Kamala Harris is also a prosecutor who put away over a thousand pot dealers still serving time. In my opinion, this president is the worst in my 67 years on this Earth, when Trump had that border almost completely secured from this problem.

I hope my story protects your children, young and old, to look for the signs of addiction and assists in making them get treatment. Call your congressman to fight for his or her rights for the treatment they deserve. Addiction is a disease, like any other. I blame the State reps, who could have made sure there were places for them to go for help instead of waiting months for beds; this would have stopped anyone facing federal prison. DA offices, and the point where the problem really came from for my son, was during the Obama and Biden administrations. Today in 2022, we have more deaths, crimes, and the worst drug problem now than we ever had. I am worried about the children in this generation more than any before. China sends the Fentanyl to Mexico cartels, and they smuggle it across our border. Teenagers can buy it on Snapchat and other sites, thinking they are getting other pills. Parents should keep their eyes on their Chat Apps. My opinion is that we need people who care and will fix this problem. Close our borders.

We need better Congress and State Officials leading this country. We also need better judges, prosecutors, lawyers, and mostly better run state and federal officials running our country. Remember, it is a disease and not a crime. Drugs are a big threat. I hope my story heals the families that lost their children to drugs.

I hope my story protects your children, young and old, to look for the signs of addiction and assists in making them get treatment. They could have made sure there were places for them to go to help instead of waiting months for beds. Today in 2023, we have more deaths, crimes, and the worst drug problem now than we ever had. I am worried about the children in this generation more than any before.

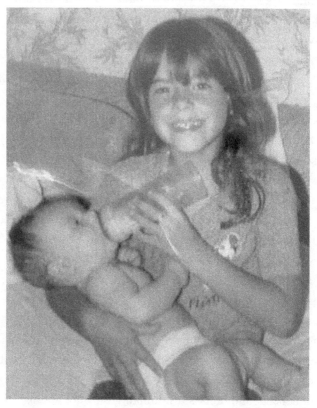

Rachael (7 years old) feeding her baby brother

Shane and Rachael Christmas Morning (1987)

Me speaking at the walk, thanking everyone for showing up.

Friends and police showed up for the walk.

My friend Maureen speaks about the loss of her son
Brandon.

Here are some of the certificates Shane accomplished:

CERTIFICATE OF ACHIEVEMENT

IS PRESENTED TO:

Shane Hansen

95415-038

Given this 8th Day of November 2017

at
United States Penitentiary, Hazelton
West Virginia

For completing the Non-Residential Drug Abuse Program.
You are commended for your participation.

M. Lardin
Drug Treatment Specialist
USP Hazelton

Psychology Services
Special Housing Unit

Certificate of Completion

to

Shane Hansen

95415-038

For Successfully Completing

Turning Point Module-
Drug Abuse

Federal Correctional Complex
United States Penitentiary
Hazelton, West Virginia

Awarded on
August 18, 2019

Dr. Cronch, Restrictive Housing
Unit Psychologist

Psychology Services Presents

Certificate of Completion

to

Shane Hansen

95415-038

For Successfully Completing:

Independent Study: "Dimensions of Change"

Special Housing Unit,
Federal Correctional Complex, United States Penitentiary
Hazelton, West Virginia

Awarded on: October 21, 2019

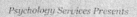

Dr. Crouch, Restrictive Housing
Unit Psychologist

Printed in the USA
CPSIA information can be obtained
at www.ICGtesting.com
LVHW091600291023
762330LV00049B/646